A sign of a profession becoming mature is when it begins to pay more attention to ethics, values and responsibilities of practitioners rather than being excited about fashionable ideas and new marketing devices. Benita Mayhead is clearly in tune with the professional maturation of the coaching field offering a book with a fresh look at the duty of care that is expected from us as coaches. Her book is a systematic exploration of duty of care as a concept and its application to practice. Not just an opinion-based text, it is supported by a wide range of relevant conceptual and research-based sources as well as her own doctoral study. It will be an important asset for a serious beginner in the coaching field whilst also challenging some unquestioned assumptions held by seasoned practitioners.

Professor Tatiana Bachkirova
International Centre for Coaching and Mentoring Studies,
Oxford Brookes University

Benita's book 'Duty of Care in Coaching' is a rigorous and thought-provoking exploration of duty of care in coaching. Grounded in empirical research and contemporary coaching theory, it offers a critical yet highly practical examination of the ethical responsibilities coaches face in their professional practice. What sets this work apart is its ability to bridge conceptual depth with real-world applicability. Benita articulates complex ethical dilemmas with clarity and precision, supporting coaches in refining their practice through evidence-based insights and reflective inquiry. Her writing is both engaging and academically robust, making this book an essential resource for those committed to coaching with integrity, responsibility, and impact. A foundational text for scholars, practitioners, and anyone invested in the ethical maturation of the coaching profession.

Dr Christine Vitzthum
CEO, 2TOP GmbH, EMCC Global Master Practitioner

Coaching of both individuals and teams have become the norm in corporate life today. This has led to an assumption of set standards for coaching as in other professions. Given the reach and impact of coaches, these certainly should be established. It is therefore refreshing to see Benita address the crucial issue of duty of care in coaching, bringing the rigour of the scientific method in her approach. In a world where anyone can profess to be an expert, her grounding in evidence elevates this to the standards the profession deserves. Adding to it the benefit of her own accomplished experience and warm tone of voice. I hope this is the first of many.

Neela Das
VP of Technology Optimisation, Elsevier (RELX)

I believe duty of care is a critical consideration for coaches and yet overlooked by some in the field. This can have a serious impact on the success of the assignment and the mental wellbeing on the coachee. I have been a client of Benita's for many years and have seen the positive impact that can be achieved when coaches consider the principles and key roles and responsibilities of duty of care from the outset. Benita has drawn upon her own learning and relevant research to shine a light on the key concepts of duty of care in her book, along with practical advice and frameworks for practitioners at every level.

David Wilson
Group Head, Risk Intelligence, LSEG

Dr Benita Mayhead's book 'Duty of Care in Coaching' is an essential and timely contribution to the coaching profession, shedding light on the often-overlooked concept of duty of care. Grounded in rigorous research and real-world insights, this book challenges coaches to reflect deeply on their ethical responsibilities and professional standards. In an increasingly complex and interconnected world, where cultural differences shape coaching relationships, the need for ethical awareness has never been greater. Benita expertly navigates these nuances, offering invaluable guidance for both new and experienced practitioners. A must-read for those committed to ethical excellence, ensuring coaching remains a responsible and transformative practice that upholds the highest standards of care across diverse contexts.

Coretta Hine
Founder CEO, Coretta Coaching & Consultancy, President EMCC UK

I am sure that Benita's evidence-based, practice-oriented book 'Duty of Care in Coaching' will become a staple companion for coaches and researchers alike. Benita discusses the concepts, theories and research findings from academic research in a highly relatable way, so any practitioner can integrate these ideas in their own practice. Benita acknowledges the duty of care dilemmas that lie in the murky grey areas of everyday coaching practice, and brings these to life with rich examples. On a personal level, I particularly enjoyed the book because I can hear Benita's voice just as it sounds in person: warm and personable, articulate and precise, and above all, interested in each individual coach's experience of duty of care in their practice.

Dr Kirsty Denyer
Lecturer in Coaching for Behavioural Change, Leadership, Organisations, Behaviour and Reputation, Henley Business School

This is a book I didn't know I needed until I started reading it. Duty of care sits at the heart of ethical coaching, yet it's something many of us, me included, haven't explored in any depth. This book changes that. Benita brings the topic to life with real-world examples and research that make it both engaging and highly relevant. What I love most are the reflective questions and exercises woven throughout each chapter. Whether you're new to coaching or have been practising for years, they challenge you to think deeply about your role and responsibilities. It's rare to find a book that balances theory and practical application so well, but Benita does just that. More than anything, this book has made me reflect on my own coaching practice, and I have no doubt it will do the same for others. A must-read for coaches at every stage.

Verity Hannell, Programme Director for the Professional Certificate in Executive Coaching at Henley Business School, British HR Coach of the Year 2022, ICF PCC

DUTY OF CARE IN COACHING

Grounded in primary and evidence-based research, this book is the first to investigate and provide guidance on navigating contemporary challenges that coaches, supervisors, educators, and organisations experience in achieving ethical best practice and legal responsibility.

This book addresses the complexities and difficulties of ensuring ethical best practice and duty of care in coaching, acting as an essential handbook for all those associated with and working in the field. Each chapter provides practical and crucial tips and insights and informs the reader on how to build ethical best practices in coaching, covering topics such as contracts and terms of engagement, setting ethical boundaries and limits, developing ethical maturity as a coach, and exploring contemporary systemic challenges in coaching.

Coaches from all disciplines in coaching, educators, supervisors, organisations using coaching, academics, and researchers will find this book an invaluable resource.

Dr. Benita Mayhead is an experienced executive coach, coaching supervisor, and facilitator of leadership development initiatives. She holds a doctorate in coaching and mentoring and lectures on ethics and duty of care in postgraduate programmes. She is a Global Master Practitioner coach with EMCC and a Chartered Fellow of the Chartered Institute of Personnel Development (CIPD). With over 30 years' experience and a background in learning and development, Benita has built a strong reputation through her expertise and impact. Alongside her private practice, Benita services as a board director for EMCC U.K. and is actively involved in helping shape and develop coaching, mentoring, and coaching supervision in today's world.

DUTY OF CARE IN COACHING

A Comprehensive Approach to Navigating the Complexities of Contemporary Practice

Dr Benita Mayhead

Routledge
Taylor & Francis Group

LONDON AND NEW YORK

Designed cover image: Getty Images

First published 2026
by Routledge
4 Park Square, Milton Park, Abingdon, Oxon OX14 4RN

and by Routledge
605 Third Avenue, New York, NY 10158

Routledge is an imprint of the Taylor & Francis Group, an informa business

© 2026 Dr Benita Mayhead

British Library Cataloguing-in-Publication Data
A catalogue record for this book is available from the British Library

ISBN: 978-1-032-82006-4 (hbk)
ISBN: 978-1-032-82005-7 (pbk)
ISBN: 978-1-003-50249-4 (ebk)

DOI: 10.4324/9781003502494

Typeset in Sitka
by Apex CoVantage, LLC

CONTENTS

FOREWORD

What is duty of care in the coaching profession? Who owns it? What does it even mean? What does it entail? These are some of the questions that come to mind when I think of the term 'duty of care' within a coaching context.

Please don't get me wrong! As an academic in this discipline of coaching, I understand that duty of care refers to the legal and ethical responsibility coaches have to ensure the safety, wellbeing, and development of their clients. As such, they are required to take reasonable steps to prevent harm, provide a safe space for the coaching, and act in the best interests of their clients. And while the enactment of duty of care, that is, the lived experience of reflecting and acting upon our duty of care, to our coachees is timeless and ubiquitous, empirically grounded research on this important issue is lacking. As such, I am thrilled to embrace this book as the first systematic, empirically grounded and practice-oriented study of its kind. Indeed, it is not only long overdue; it is wholeheartedly welcome.

This book offers a comprehensive analysis of the multifaceted concept of duty of care in coaching, providing readers with eye-opening insights that are both thought-provoking and widely beneficial. It begins with an overview of ethical standards in coaching (Chapter 1) before delving into the crucial importance of establishing a (shared) definition of duty of care (Chapter 2). A strong emphasis is placed on both the necessity of setting and maintaining professional boundaries and standards (Chapter 3), as well as the complexities involved in contracting, especially when multiple parties are engaged in the coaching process (Chapter 4). The book then turns to two particularly significant and under-researched areas. First, it examines the evolving nature of a coach's 'duty *to* care' – an ethical and emotional dimension shaped by the coach's own values, beliefs, and experiences, which, if unchecked, can lead to the potential risk of *over-caring* (Chapter 5). Second, it explores the coach's responsibility in effectively managing the conclusion of coaching relationships, a vital yet often overlooked aspect of their duty of care to clients (Chapter 6). Further, the book engages with contemporary and pressing topics, including the coach's duty of care to the wider system in which they operate (Chapter 7), as well as the indispensable role of coaching supervision in upholding professional standards and ethical practice (Chapter 8). The reading journey concludes with a reflective and practical exploration of key takeaways (Chapter 9), alongside a transparent analysis of the theoretical and methodological foundations that underpin the book's insights. For a comprehensive chapter-by-chapter breakdown, please refer to the following Introduction.

Dr. Benita Mayhead is the ideal author to tackle this critical subject. With years of dedicated research into duty of care in coaching as part of her doctoral thesis, she has demonstrated both exceptional rigor and deep sensitivity in exploring this vital topic. Her ground-breaking study is poised to influence the discourse on ethical coaching practice for years to come. In this book, Benita has masterfully blended her scholarly expertise with her extensive experience as a distinguished executive coach and coach supervisor in order to craft an accessible and insightful guide for professional coaches, their clients, and their organisational sponsors. Academics and professional training instructors, I trust, will also find this work as enlightening, invaluable, and reassuring as I have found it.

I wish you, the reader, an enjoyable and rewarding reading and learning journey as you navigate this book.

Dr Ioanna Iordanou
Oxford Brookes Business School

ACKNOWLEDGEMENTS

Thank you for arriving here, hopefully with curiosity and interest in the subject of duty of care in coaching. I hope you enjoy the read ahead. But first, why the cover design? We find there is an intricate balance of movement as we navigate through the complexity of duty of care in our roles as coaches, mentors, and coaching supervisors. The topic of duty of care is hugely complex, nebulous and hard to pin down at times, dynamic and ever changing in the eyes of the practitioner as each situation is completely unique. The murmuration image of starlings taking to the sky captured that.

Let me introduce myself: I am an executive coach and a coaching supervisor and have been working with leaders for many decades. Between 2019 and 2022 I conducted research for a professional doctorate in coaching and mentoring at Oxford Brookes University. My topic was 'duty of care in executive coaching' (more on that throughout the book).

However, if you had said to the teenage girl who left school at 16 years old, with only a couple of exams and no real career prospects, that she'd complete a doctorate and then go on to publish a book, I don't think she would have believed you. That girl was me. Higher education wasn't an option available for me at 16. So, the road to achieving academic qualifications took a different path, one which I found later in life. It's been a long one, yet somehow, here we are. As I always a say – commitment, hard work, and a big dollop of determination go a long way.

The achievement was made possible by some incredible people who have supported and encouraged both the research and the writing of this book. Dr Ioanna Iordanou has been a constant source of inspiration and support since 2017 through my master's, then the doctorate through 2019 to 2022, and now the book. Her generosity with time and feedback has been so valued, and I am truly grateful to have her not only as a leading academic voice in the field but also as a friend.

Oxford Brookes University has a distinguished faculty. As the doctorate in coaching and mentoring cohort of 2019, we really did have the best faculty – thank you, Professor Tatiana Bachkirova, Dr Sylwia Ciuk, Dr Elaine Cox, Dr Christian Ehrlich, Dr Judie Gannon, Dr Ioanna Iordanou, Dr Peter Jackson, Professor Peter Lugosi, Dr Joanna Molyn, and Dr Adrian Myers. Thank you to Associate Professor Pauline Fatien, my examiner for the doctorate, who continues to inspire and develop the thinking in the field.

Throughout the doctorate, I got to know and truly appreciate the wisdom, academic brilliance, and support of my 'research buddy' (as we fondly called each other) – Dr Christine Vitzthum. We may have been miles apart, with Christine in Germany and me in the UK, yet we worked in parallel along our individual research projects and against the backdrop of the raging COVID-19 pandemic. We formed a close bond and connection, one that is built on trust, friendship and respect, and one that will continue for life. Thank you, my friend.

The book would not be here if it had not been for the executive coaches who volunteered to be participants in the original research. I am grateful to you all for your honesty in sharing of your experiences, and for your trust. Paramount to me throughout has been *my* duty of care to all of you and doing justice to your accounts, which should be evident in the pages ahead.

Asking for feedback on the manuscript drafts throughout writing the book has been a vital ingredient which has helped bring the concepts to life, provide sense checking, and challenge the thinking. With utmost gratitude, I'd like to share my appreciation for Neela Das, Professor Tatiana Bachkirova, Dr Kirsty Denyer, Caroline Duncan, Bec Evans, Dr Sebastian Fox, Dr Judie Gannon, Asha Ghosh, Verity Hannell, Paul Heardman, Coretta Hine, Dr Ioanna Iordanou, Dr Andrea Kilpatrick, Dr Christine Vitzthum, David Wilson, and Angela Wright. As reviewers or endorsers, all of you have helped shape the final manuscript. Thank you for your insights, experience, knowledge, support, and time. There are too many to individually mention, but please know, dear colleagues, clients, friends, and family who have asked along the way and have been interested, I am so grateful to you all.

And to my girlfriends – strong, independent, fun-loving, and kind women. Thank you for listening to me over the years, and for the encouragement both in and out of the tougher times life has managed to throw at us – Annette D'Abreo, Chloe Eichhorn, Emma Turnbull, Gina Paskins, Dr Jennifer Potts, Julia Lutterloch, Karen Gaines, Lisa Pollard, Natalie Horton, Philippa Charlton, Puni Amin, Tracey Bannister, and Victoria Pullinger. And to Julie Sneath – you said the book would be written, my beautiful friend, and you were right.

My dear mum, you will be undoubtedly proud, and in years gone by would have read the book, something my brother Justin and I know in our hearts, just as we know how proud you have always been of us both, having brought us up with very little and through challenging times. Thanks, mum.

Finally, thank you to my daughters Chloe and Eve and my husband and best friend, Anthony. Writing a book was something on the lifetime achievement list, a legacy. Ant, your belief in me and constant reassurance have been my anchor. To Chloe and Eve, thank you, darling girls, for willing me on, for your kindness, and for always reminding me what truly matters. The reinforcement from you all of 'you've got this' has stayed with me. All of this was made possible by your love, support, and belief in me. Thank you, and I love you all.

Introduction

Welcome

Welcome to this book written for coaches, coach supervisors, mentors, organisations who use coaching, providers of coach education and training, those undertaking coaching qualifications, and those concerned with setting and maintaining industry standards.

As this book attests, duty of care in coaching is not widely talked about. We have an opportunity to collectively shape the narrative and bring this important topic into the light. The research which underpins this book found an often-repeated comment by participants in the study when asked what duty of care meant to them – 'this is the first time I've thought about it'. This is not to say coaches do not think about ethical practice and duty of care; rather, it is an indication that duty of care is not clear or explicit.

This book provides a needed opportunity for a pause and reflection to explore our understanding of duty of care and our fulfilment and application of it. As you read it, whatever your background or interest in the subject, you are invited to step into the thinking, challenge previously held assumptions, and question your own understanding of what it means to have a duty of care in the work we do, and how you show it. What lies ahead comprises discussions and interpretation of the meaning of duty of care and how duty of care is enacted, such as through setting boundaries and standards, through contracting and endings. These interpretations have been developed phenomenologically through the lived experiences of coaches. The original research which underpins this book is shared throughout the book. The participants who took part in the research remain anonymous, and pseudonyms have been used where quotes and accounts from them are shared.

The motivation for writing the book comes from my own curiosity about how fellow coaches make sense of duty of care and the implications of practice relating to matters of ethics when coaching. Primary empirical research on ethics and duty of care in coaching has been lacking-a vital element

DOI: 10.4324/9781003502494-1

which has been missing from the theoretical foundations that underpin our work. Having spent several decades working with leaders and teams, I have experienced first-hand the complex nature of the work we do in our field and recognise that when finding ourselves in an ethical dilemma, a policy or a code of ethics rarely guides us through. For me as an executive coach, the value of coaching supervision becomes especially important when I find myself in a tricky situation and, more broadly, in reflecting on and refining my practice. The relationship with a supervisor plays a vital role in my own coaching practice, one which continues to shape and guide me as a practitioner. We are never the finished article in our development; there is always room to learn and grow. My aim is for this book to be another piece in the jigsaw puzzle of our own ongoing development and to offer a contribution to our world of coaching to further develop our thinking.

Before the study that forms the basis of this book (Mayhead, 2022), virtually no primary research had taken place to explore how coaches make sense of and enact their duty of care. It is a complex, nuanced, and nebulous topic, perhaps part of the reason we don't have much empirical research on it. My own curiosity and desire to make a positive impact and an informed, evidence-based contribution to the field was strong, and, coupled with a sense of determination, the research study was born. I also had voices I valued around me, in particular Dr Ioanna Iordanou, whose book I refer to many times in the pages ahead (Iordanou, Hawley and Iordanou, 2017). Ioanna was my director of studies during my professional doctorate, and her knowledge, challenges, support, and understanding of ethics helped me raise the bar on the research I will now be sharing with you. My contribution to you, as the reader, is a snapshot of the years of work, re-worded into practical reflections, to help shape and develop your own understanding.

Terms used in this book

Various terms are used throughout the chapters ahead, and I'd like to take a moment here to offer some descriptions. Duty of care is referenced many times. It is part of the ethical framework of conduct in how a coach acts and is associated with the coach's own sense of what is fair and right, both legally and ethically, connected to the coach's own principles of behaviour (Iordanou et al., 2017). This underscores how crucial it is for coaches to continually polish the mirror of their own self-awareness. In its legal form, duty of care relates to an obligation for someone not to cause harm to others. In the chapters that follow we will spend time delving into the meaning in actual practice, bringing duty of care and ethics off the page and into our day-to-day thinking as practitioners. We perhaps tend to use the term ethics quite broadly, and it is indeed an expansive topic.

I reference the 'coach', 'client', and 'customer' throughout the book. The coach is the practitioner, and you can also think of this as being a mentor or coaching supervisor, as many of the principles discussed in the book will apply. The client is the person being coached, and this may be singular or multiple, for example, if the coach is working with a team. The customer has several meanings. It refers to the sponsor of the coaching, such the organisation that may have commissioned the work and, most often, is paying for the service. Yet when coaching is pro bono, for no fee, there is still a customer. It also refers to key stakeholders in the coaching relationship, for example, human resources, talent development, or the client's line manager. More broadly, the customer could be team members the client may be working with or their direct reports.

'Coaching bodies' are referred to, and these are the professional organisations that offer membership and/or accreditation/credentialling to practitioners. The largest coaching bodies currently are the International Coaching Federation (ICF), European Mentoring and Coaching Council (EMCC), and Association for Coaching (AC), and there are also many smaller ones.

The current landscape

Before we probe the depths of duty of care, let's take a quick step back and survey the coaching landscape we currently find ourselves in. The coaching market is the second-fastest growing sector in business and was given an estimated value in excess of $2 billion in 2019 (Hawkins and Turner, 2019); yet more recent ICF data from 2022 estimates it at over $4 billion. The supply is also on a continued growth trajectory with record numbers of new coaches emerging, yet coaching is unregulated, with no single governing body. Although the coaching bodies, including the ICF, EMCC, AC, and others, have competency frameworks (Brennan and Wildflower, 2018), they operate independently of each other. That said, they have gone some way towards uniting by way of introducing the Global Code of Ethics, first written by the AC and EMCC and launched in 2016. Today, this code has many signatories. The ICF continues to operate under its own code of ethics.

The number of coaches is growing, with many striving to fulfil coaching body accreditation. Applications for accreditation focus mostly on skill and competence, with coaches graded on their level of experience based on frameworks, yet these are as yet unsubstantiated as a means of assessing coaching capabilities (Bachkirova and Smith, 2015). Being a member of, or accredited by, one of the coaching bodies may help increase the professional credibility of a coach (Iordanou et al., 2017). Whilst coaching is unregulated, coaches who are members of or accredited by a coaching body agree to abide by the relevant guidelines and principles for that body. What percentage this is of total coach practitioners is unknown. Regardless of whether the coach is accredited or a member of a coaching body, they must still uphold the laws of common law jurisdictions.

Early literature raised concerns about the quality of coach training pro-grammes in response to poorly trained coaches (Bluckert, 2006). A shift occurred as the industry responded with reports of 52% of customers (those buying coaching) requiring coaches to be credentialled by a coaching body (PwC, 2007). The last decade has witnessed further moves towards coach training, including an emerging narrative about coaches needing to first understand themselves before working with others (Atad and Grant, 2021). Since our coaching is a reflection of who we are as a person, we are seeing more focus in the literature on both professional and personal development (Bachkirova, 2016).

We are seeing an increase in membership applications to coaching bodies, and the trend of clients requiring coaching body membership or accredita-tion when appointing a coach continues to grow. Nearly all coach practi-tioners surveyed by ICF in the Global Coaching Study (2020) unsurprisingly reported having completed some coach-specific training, with 93% of the training having been accredited or approved through a coaching body. However, to what degree ethics, or indeed duty of care, are featured in the training is unknown. I urge coaches to be vigilant in exploring the content of training when making choices on where to qualify and interrogate the detail of what will be covered in the training. We must remind ourselves that coaching qualifications (such as a qualification that could lead to a certifi-cate, diploma, or master's, for example) are not the same as coaching body membership/accreditation/credentialling. The two are different.

For a coach, fostering wellbeing and mental health awareness is a funda-mental responsibility that extends beyond performance and skill develop-ment. A coach holds a significant position of trust and influence, and this comes with a responsibility to recognise the needs of those we are working with, including the most extreme situations of suicide. This is a complex and sensitive realm we may find ourselves in, and coaches have a responsibility to equip themselves with the knowledge and awareness to recognise – not to diagnose – potential issues but to know how to offer support, signpost, and get access to appropriate resources for the client when necessary. This is arguably absent from many coach training programmes. How much atten-tion is given to mental health awareness and wellbeing in coach training, and whether coaches are being adequately prepared to address these critical areas, remains unclear. The aim of this book is not to analyse or compare the content and quality of coach training but to shine a light specifically on the complexity of duty of care and our roles and responsibilities and how to operate ethically and within the law of our common law jurisdictions.

Background

Let me start by providing an insight into the background of how this book came to be, an insight into the doctoral research that led to the writing of the book, the reasons it is needed, and why *now*. Interrogation of the literature showed that duty of care in coaching was not explored as much as it is in other related helping professions such as counselling and psychotherapy, or even sports coaching. Instead, duty of care has been buried in nuance and assumption, not explicitly referenced in codes of ethics, and has remained quietly in the ethical frameworks (Mayhead, 2022).

The research study which forms the basis of this book was conducted between 2019 and 2022, and the research explored the meaning of duty of care in coaching and coaches' perceptions of how they enact it (Mayhead, 2022). This was the first empirical study, as previous research had been concerned with how coaches navigate ethical dilemmas and only from the perspective of coaches who had accreditation or were members of a coaching body. The coaches who took part in my research were a combination of some who had coaching body membership and some who did not. This is an important point, as the findings demonstrated that regardless of coaching body affiliation, accreditation, or membership, all coaches have a duty of care in the work they do, yet few participants could articulate what that actually meant. This book enables coaches and those working in the coaching field to develop a clearer sense of what duty of care means and to consider how it is demonstrated.

Failure to pay attention to and understand our duty of care as practitioners can lead to serious consequences. For the coach, this might include legal implications if negligence or actions cause harm or if there is a breach of contract or professional standards. Additional consequences could include reputational damage and the loss of accreditation or credentials from a coaching body. Working with other human beings, coaches are in privileged roles, and they can have profound influence on a client's wellbeing and the outcomes they aim to achieve. Neglecting this duty not only risks causing harm to the client or those in the coaching relationship but also undermines trust and the potential for meaningful client development.

My research resulted in several findings and contributions, one of which was the development of a definition of duty of care in coaching, which we shall explore in Chapter 2. The definition is an important element, as it forms the foundation of where the book then travels to. Yet some readers might argue that a definition is not necessary and that a definition could lead to an oversimplification of duty of care. This is indeed a worthy challenge. If we could arrive at agreement on a few words for such a complex topic (as we shall explore), have we not then missed the point entirely? Instead, the definition is offered to help untangle the complexity and arrange the component elements in such a way that we might use them as a development tool moving us from horizontal to vertical development rather than something to put a tick box next to.

How to use this book

The book is structured to either move from chapter to chapter in chronological order or to take each chapter separately. The next section of this Introduction provides an overview of each chapter and ends with an exercise. You are invited to complete this exercise at the start of reading the book and again afterwards.

Chapter 1 – Duty of care in coaching; shifting sands of change

Coaching is still a relatively young field and has drawn much from related helping professions in how it has been shaped and developed thus far. In this chapter I share how our understanding of duty of care has been informed from these related professional contexts, and we will delve into its legal and ethical dimensions. The role of codes of ethics and the need for our awareness of standards are explored before drawing attention to how codes and standards cannot provide all of the answers. Finally, we will pause to consider how the shifting sands of technology and AI are moving with increased rapidity and how this has significant and consequential implications for our duty of care.

Chapter 2 – Building understanding of duty of care in coaching

This chapter tackles the debate of whether duty of care in coaching should, or should not, be defined and positions the argument and reasoning about why we do need a definition. Colourful illustrations from coaches are shared on what has shaped their understanding of duty of care. These illustrations include stories and experiences about role models coaches have encountered, life experiences, and their own development. We then explore a definition, followed by a detailed exercise where we can explore what duty of care means to us, helping develop our own understanding of it further.

Chapter 3 – Boundaries and standards in coaching

Chapter 3 brings attention to how duty of care is enacted and this includes the coach being responsible for setting the standards and boundaries in the coaching relationship, irrespective of size and whether coaches are providing coaching services with or without fees. The chapter discusses the merits of having such standards in place before conducting work, as they act as a safeguard for all those in the coaching relationship. This also has relevance for external coaches who might be working in a quasi-internal coaching role and for in-house coaches.

Chapter 4 – Contracting as a coach

Coaches identify with contracting as being part of how they enact their duty of care. Best practice informs us that contracting between the coach and client is essential, and Chapter 4 develops this by exploring how the coach can navigate the intricacies of contracting with multiple parties in the coaching relationship. This chapter offers practical guidance for how to manage contracting, which is also vital for the in-house coach. Setting terms of agreement for the work can assist in ensuring clarity of expectations, and this chapter provides suggestions for what might be included.

Chapter 5 – Care and coaching; developing ethical maturity

This chapter turns our attention to the lived experiences of coaches and a further key finding from the research of coaches' having a duty *to* care, born from their values and beliefs, and how this forms part of their development of ethical maturity. Coaches develop a 'duty *to* care' for the work they do, but this can also be fraught with the danger of over-caring. In this part of the book, we'll explore how the coach might safeguard against this, including how they maintain boundaries, and we'll discuss the ongoing cycle of developing ethical maturity.

Chapter 6 – Endings in coaching

Literature from psychology and related fields informs us that endings are important for human beings, yet coaches are not always well versed in managing them. Part of coaches' responsibility, and another element of their perception of how they enact duty of care, includes working with the client/customer towards endings in the coaching relationship. This also applies to in-house coaches and coaches working in a quasi-internal role. Chapter 6 discusses why this is important and how we can move towards the co-creation of good-enough endings. The chapter also explores the pitfalls to be avoided and offers insight into why coaching is not always ended.

Chapter 7 – Adopting a systemic lens for duty of care in coaching

Chapter 7 discusses how today's coaches have contemporary challenges to deal with in relation to the multiple stakeholders in coaching relationships and how adopting a systemic lens to our duty of care can support us. As an example, the external coach is contracted to work within an organisation, and as a minimum there is the coach, the person being coached or the team (the client), and the organisation or the bill payer (the customer) in the relationship. This chapter presents phenomenologically informed perspectives from coaches' own lived experiences about to whom we have a duty of care.

Chapter 8 – Coaching supervision; navigating the rifts and tensions

Dependent on who is asked, coaching supervision may be considered as a necessity or a nicety. I have already shared the importance and value I find from it. Aside from personal preference, this chapter dives into research evidencing that coaches seek reflective dialogue, primarily with their coaching supervisor, when navigating ethical dilemmas. In this chapter we'll consider the vital importance of coaching supervision and explore how the coach can expect an increase in complexity of case load as they develop and grow in their own coaching practice. This chapter challenges coaching bodies' positions and places coaching supervision firmly in the coach's practice, demonstrating how the more experienced the coach, the greater the need for supervision. It is crucial that as coaches we must take care of ourselves, and put our own oxygen masks on first, before we can work with others. The chapter ends with how supervision can act as a restorative resource.

Chapter 9 – Bringing it together; putting good practice in to practice

Throughout the book the reader is offered questions and exercises to help with their development and understanding of ethics and duty of care. This penultimate chapter serves as a culmination of the book's key concepts, guiding the reader through exercises designed to deepen understanding and application of the material in the book. The reader is offered an opportunity to engage with what they've learned and examine their own coaching, mentoring, or supervision practice, putting good practice into practice.

Chapter 10 – Research overview

For those interested in the research that underpins this book, Chapter 10 offers an insight into the literature review and the methodology. The literature review comprised first an interrogation of all systematic and meta-analyses of literature reviews in coaching conducted between 2009 and 2021. These are listed, and an overview of the main themes found is shared before moving into the main body of the literature review, which explored ethics and duty of care in coaching, related helping professions, and sports coaching. The chapter gives an overview of the research methodology, which was underpinned by a constructivist research paradigm, and the qualitative and inductive approach adopted. Also provided is a snapshot of the analysis conducted across the 30 interviews conducted and the scrutiny used.

Concluding thoughts

We need to discuss duty of care and ethics within the coaching field, which continues to expand globally. Across the multiple genres of coaching, from executive to personal development, to coaching in specific sectors such as education and health care, to team or pro bono coaching, there is a pressing requirement for coaches and those involved in the coaching community to pause and reflect on their duty of care and the legal and ethical responsibilities towards themselves, their clients, and the wider systems. We hold a privileged role of responsibility in the work we do with fellow human beings, and stopping to consider the known and unknown ripple effect of our actions will help our development and understanding.

Not only do we have the multiple genres of coaching, we also have cultural differences. Coaching practices and the ethical dilemmas coaches may experience vary from culture to culture, influenced by social norms, values, and expectations from society, the client, and the coach. As an example, differences arise between adopting more egalitarian and collaborative approaches in some cultures and an appreciation of hierarchy and less challenge or questioning in others. Approaches to conflict differ across the globe, with some cultures being more conflict averse and others more conflict tolerant. We must also consider the maturity of coaching in areas of the world where coaching is less established and the development of professional boundaries and clear ethical standards is in its infancy. I invite readers to reflect on this and bring the unique context and diversity of each situation and relationship into their thinking. Each situation and relationship will be intricately exclusive.

My aim is not to generalise, and this book is not about dissecting cultural difference. Instead, it offers an opportunity to pause and comes with an invitation for coaches, mentors and coaching supervisors to critically reflect on the multifaceted, complex nature of duty of care and the contemporary challenges we are experiencing. The book aims to inform understanding of duty of care in coaching, setting the stage for further in-depth exploration and helping to ensure ethical practice and wellbeing of all those involved in coaching relationships. While the book cannot provide all the answers for resolving every ethical dilemma, it serves as a guide to help deepen our understanding of ourselves. By reflecting on what is presented ahead, we can better navigate the complexities of ethical challenges, fostering our own personal growth and development in the process.

It starts with us.

Your practice in focus

Based on your current knowledge and experience, take a moment to reflect on the following questions before continuing with this book. As a suggestion, I encourage you to undertake this exercise both at the beginning and on finishing reading the book, allowing yourself time to observe any changes in your perspectives. In true coaching style, perhaps journal your thinking, or take a step outside and walk as you reflect on the prompts.

'What does duty of care mean to me in my role?'

Take a few moments to write down what the term 'duty of care' means to you personally and professionally. Consider how this aligns with your core values and responsibilities. Reflect on how your definition might differ from common or legal definitions and why this might be.

'What has helped shape and influence my understanding of duty of care?'

Reflect on experiences, events, or situations that have impacted your perception of duty of care. Perhaps this includes formal training or education, personal or professional experiences, or challenging situations you have encountered. What impact have these had on your understanding?

'Who has helped shape and influence my understanding of duty of care?'

Think about the individuals who have played a key role in shaping your perspective on duty of care. It may be a person or a characteristic of someone you have known. They might have been a family member, colleague, friend, mentor, or someone from your professional career. Reflect on what it was that influenced you.

'What is it that I do to demonstrate my duty of care?'

Reflect on the specific actions or behaviours that demonstrate your duty of care in your daily work. Consider both the routine practices and what happens when you find yourself with unexpected challenges.

'How do I continue to develop my own sense of understanding of duty of care?'

Reflect on the ways you can continue to develop and evolve your understanding and enactment of duty of care. Perhaps this is through professional development, education, reflective practice, or supervi-sion. What would help you develop further?

Take a moment to review your responses and reflect on how your understanding of duty of care has evolved over time. Think about how you can repeat this exercise periodically to see how your perceptions have changed and how your practice continues to develop.

Enjoy the read ahead.

References

Atad, O. and Grant, A. (2021) 'How does coach training change coaches-in-training? Differential effects for novice vs. experienced "skilled help-ers"', *Coaching: An International Journal of Theory, Research and Practice*, 14(1), pp. 3–19. https://doi.org/10.1080/17521882.2019.1707246

Bachkirova, T. (2016) 'The self of the coach: Conceptualization, issues, and opportunities for practitioner development', *Consulting Psychology Journal: Practice and Research*, 68(2), pp. 143–156. https://doi.org/10.1037/cpb0000055

Bachkirova, T. and Smith, C. (2015) 'From competencies to capabilities in the assessment and accreditation of coaches', *International Journal of Evidence Based Coaching and Mentoring*, 13(2), pp. 123–140. https://doi.org/10.24384/IJEBCM

Bluckert, P. (2006) *Psychological dimensions of executive coaching*. UK: McGraw-Hill Education.

Brennan, D. and Wildflower, L. (2018) 'Ethics in coaching', In *The complete handbook of coaching*, eds. E. Cox, T. Bachkirova, and D. Clutterbuck. 3rd Ed. London: Sage. pp. 500–517.

Hawkins, P. and Turner, E. (2019) *Systemic coaching: Delivering value beyond the individual*. UK: Routledge. doi.org/10.1037/1061-4087.55.2.94

ICF Global Coaching Study (2020) International Coaching Federation (ICF). https://coachingfederation.org/app/uploads/2020/09/FINAL_ICF_GCS 2020_ExecutiveSummary.pdf

Iordanou, I., Hawley, R. and Iordanou, C. (2017) *Values and ethics in coaching*. London: Sage. https://doi.org/10.4135/9781473983755

Mayhead, B. (2022) 'Duty of care in coaching: From ethical frameworks to the development of the coach', Doctoral thesis. Oxford Brookes University. https://doi.org/10.24384/sjmq-9b67

PwC (2007) *ICF global coaching study*. Lexington, KY: International Coach Federation.

1 Duty of care in coaching

Shifting sands of change

Introduction

Welcome to Chapter 1, where the groundwork begins on forming our understanding of duty of care in coaching. To help us navigate through this expansive topic, the chapter starts by exploring the meaning of duty of care in related professional contexts before moving on to duty of care in coaching, codes of ethics, and the impact of the ever-shifting sands of technology and artificial intelligence (AI) in coaching. Exploring how other mature professions have developed their sense of duty of care helps us towards a rounded understanding of the concept and the concomitant legalities and to form our own appreciation of the concept in coaching. In Chapter 2 we will build on this understanding with a definition for duty of care in coaching.

Duty of care in related professional contexts

Let's start by exploring what we know about duty of care in related professional contexts. As coaching is considered a relatively young field, and as our knowledge thus far has been shaped in large part from related helping professions, it makes sense to start there. Also, it is evident from the literature that, unlike in other related helping professions, duty of care in coaching has not been clearly defined (Bond, 2015). In Chapter 2, I will offer you a definition of duty of care for coaching, but for now, let's start with building the jigsaw puzzle of how our knowledge has been informed to date.

We have drawn much from related helping professions, in particular from counselling and psychotherapy, in forming knowledge and practice in coaching. Both have steadily established a shared understanding of ethical conduct that goes beyond professional duties to include all facets of human interaction (Iordanou, Hawley and Iordanou, 2017). Counselling and psychotherapy codes of practice include common themes of doing no harm and acting in ways that promote the welfare of others. Iordanou et al. (2017)

DOI: 10.4324/9781003502494-2

mention how practitioners in these fields are required to work within their scope of competence and how they are to respect the interests of their client and the law. In counselling, duty of care is defined as a 'legal term for a personal or social responsibility to someone that forms the basis for liability in negligence when not fulfilled' (Bond, 2015, p. 306).

In nursing, duty of care has different meanings, dependent on whether it relates to a legal or to a professional duty of care (Royal College of Nursing, 2020). Discharging a legal duty of care requires nursing practitioners to act in accordance with the relevant standard of care. Discharging a professional duty of care requires the nursing practitioner to follow codes and guidance policy. Indeed, what constitutes duty of care has also been a topic much debated in medical law since the landmark Montgomery case (*Montgomery (Appellant) v Lanarkshire Health Board (Respondent)*, 2015). This case radically changed what had been the doctrine of a doctor's practice, the Bolam principle (*Bolam vs Friern Health Management Committee*, 1957), to a law which now requires a doctor to focus on what a patient would want to know. This was a move toward patient-centred care, away from the logical analysis of the Bolam principle to greater disclosure of information for the patient.

In other fields, sports coaching has experienced a shift in focus on duty of care in recent years. In sports coaching, it is generally understood that a sports coach has a responsibility to ensure the wellbeing and safety of those they oversee (Partington, 2016). The sports coach has a responsibility to apply appropriate skill and care to prevent those under their supervision from facing unnecessary or unacceptable risks, given the specific circumstances (Partington, 2016). The argument for education and training of sports coaches in matters relating to duty of care features in the literature, with dialogue now turning much more to its importance (Partington, 2017, 2021).

Indeed, sports coaches find themselves in an area where the field of negligence is fraught with difficulty in predicting what constitutes conduct that is deemed negligent. The sports coach works with behavioural elements. A focus on the need for sports coaches to protect those they coach, both physically and psychologically, has been promoted in recent years. This urgency has been driven by growing awareness of issues such as mental health, safeguarding, and the long-term impact of both physical and emotional harm in sports.

We can find similarities and differences between sports coaching and our own world of coaching. The sports coach addresses psychological and behavioural elements such as developing collaboration skills or trust and teamwork. This is beyond merely technical skills but related to how the sports coach develops the individual as a whole (Iordanou, 2018). It is suggested that sports coaches are responsible for establishing a moral climate – an environment where the coach positively influences what is happening, with the sports coach having a responsibility to themselves and to act as moral agents both on and off the pitch or field or whatever sporting arena they are working in (Garratt, Piper and Taylor, 2013; Lyle, 2019). So it is not just about the sports coaching session but the entire environment the sports coach creates for the team or individuals they are coaching.

However, in coaching, the same principles regarding the latter element do not completely apply. A coach does not have a 'positive obligation' to 'promote the welfare' of those they work with, as this would extend beyond the coach's professional role and could cause undue liability. Coaches in the context of this book do have a duty of care to avoid causing harm, but requiring them to 'ensure' wellbeing, or 'promote wellbeing' or personal safety, could make the coach responsible for issues outside of their expertise. Unlike medical professionals, counselling, psychotherapy, or sports coaches, coaches in the context of this book don't have exactly the same obligation.

Legal and ethical dimensions

Whilst the legal principles referred to in this book relate to the law in the United Kingdom, interrogation of the literature provides confidence that the legal principles that form the foundation of negligence are generally consistent across most common law jurisdictions (Partington, 2021). We have a responsibility, however, to understand for ourselves what applies and to work accordingly within the legal requirements of the common law jurisdiction we may be in.

Coaching is unregulated and without universal standards. Coaches do not necessarily always have written agreements, nor is there always a requirement for agreements to be in writing, although best practice would be to have the agreements written down (Wright and O'Connor, 2021). However, the law of contract applies whether terms are in writing or not. A contract is a legally binding promise, either written or verbal, by one party to fulfil an obligation to another party in return for payment in any form.

Duty of care encompasses both legal and ethical dimensions in professional contexts and is described as being part of the ethical framework of conduct (Iordanou et al., 2017). A coach's duty of care is a legal obligation, requiring their 'adherence to a standard of reasonable care' in relation to any acts that could cause harm (Wright and O'Connor, 2021). Although coaches do not have specific laws relating to coaching, they are required to adhere to the general law of civil liability, the common law of tort (Mitchels and Bond, 2010). Common law of tort is a branch of law that imposes civil liability for breaches of obligations or civil wrongs which occur when someone fails to act as a reasonable person would, resulting in harm or loss to another (Williams, 2006). This can include negligence – doing something a person who is considered to be reasonable would refrain from doing if they were in a similar, or the same, situation (Williams, 2006). This applies to all coaches, regardless of their coaching body membership status.

In the event of a claim in negligence, a court would want to consider all circumstances of the case, including the contract and the scope of the coach's duty. Consideration would be given to whether the required standard of care owed by the coach was given and whether a duty was breached (Wright and O'Connor, 2021). Regardless of whether there are written agreements, it is likely the court would want to hear what a prudent practitioner would have done, given the same scenario (Wright and O'Connor, 2021). In circumstances where a claim in negligence is brought, it would need to be determined whether a duty of care was owed. Four elements are typically required for a claim in negligence, including the presence of a legal duty not to cause harm, failure to live up to that duty, the breach has legally caused loss, and the claimant has suffered damage (Wright and O'Connor, 2021).

There are few examples of claims in negligence which have been brought against coaches. Complaints can be raised to professional coaching bodies, and these are typically investigated and managed in-house, and details are not available in public domains. Nor do we hear of legal cases. That's not to say they aren't happening, only that we are not able to compile reliable data on them. It is crucial that we equip ourselves as practitioners, that we understand both the legalities and the ethical considerations, and that we explore the meaning and potential implications for ourselves.

In addition to the legal obligations, the coach is also required to make ethical decisions, and how they develop their ethical maturity in relation to this requirement is important. In coaching, as in other related fields, duty of care applies not only to the legalities but also to the ethical and moral elements of a coach's practice (Iordanou et al., 2017). The literature argues that several factors contribute to a coach's selection of an ethical course of action. These are the coach's individual character, their training in ethics, their moral reasoning, and how they identify with the coaching profession (Williams, 2006).

Evident in my own research was how, as coaches, we associate duty of care with our own sense of what is fair and what is right through our own moral reasoning, connected to our own principles of behaviour, values, and life experiences (Mayhead, 2022). Furthermore, duty of care is omnipresent, continually there. It encompasses all interactions of the coach (Iordanou et al., 2017). The coach's duty of care is ever present and applies at all times and is not limited to specific moments.

More specifically, it covers the protection of a coach and their clients. It is concerned with morality in relation to others and safeguarding the practitioner and those they work with. Fundamentally, it relates to doing no harm to oneself or to others (Torda, 2005; Garratt et al., 2013; Bond, 2015). It is for us to explore and understand the legal obligations in our common law jurisdictions and the ethical obligation in our roles.

Coach development in ethics

Ethics is conceptualised as a developmental process, and literature from related helping professions suggests that ethical reasoning improves through professional training (Carroll and Shaw, 2013). Nevertheless, most of the coaches interviewed in my own research did not cite ethics training as a factor in their own ethical development or in their understanding of duty of care (Mayhead, 2022). My research findings suggest that coaches do not actively use ethics training or codes of ethics to support their ethical development as practitioners. Their experiences of coach training revealed that limited attention was given to ethics and legalities, with insufficient focus on developing these areas during their training. Furthermore, whilst coaching bodies' codes of ethics provide frameworks for coaches to follow, coaches' development in ethics and how they make sense of duty of care happen through reflexive practice in coaching supervision, dialogue with their peers, and looking back at past life experiences. This is evident across coaches, both those who are members of coaching bodies and those who are not (Mayhead, 2022).

In coaching literature, limited research has been conducted on what coach training providers offer and how ethics – more specifically duty of care – features in their offerings. Coach training organisations operate within unregulated commercial markets, and there have been calls for all coach training providers to be qualified. With no regulation, coach training providers are free to design and deliver highly valuable training to meet the needs of the market (Hawkins and Turner, 2019). In an ICF member survey, 99% of coach practitioners reported they had completed some coach-specific training (unsurprisingly), with 93% of coach training programmes offered by accredited/approved coaching organisations (ICF Global Coaching Study, 2020). Yet the depth of ethics and duty of care included in these programmes is unknown. Certain standards must be met for accreditation as a training provider or coach. For example, the first ICF core competency is 'demonstrates ethical practice'. That said, it is interesting that there is a lack of reference back to coach training when coaches reflect on where their knowledge on ethics comes from (Mayhead, 2022).

One of the requirements for accreditation of a coaching body is demonstration of a certain number of hours in coach training. For example, 60 hours of training is required by the ICF for the entry level. With a swathe of coach training providers on the market, it is impossible to provide robust data on the quality or content of the training. Internet searches provide an insight into the varying options available to coaches – from university-backed academic coach qualifications to alarming programmes of 'how to become a coach in one day'. It goes without saying that coach training bearing the approved badge of a coaching body must meet the requirements of said coaching body, with ethics being part of the training, but to what depth and breadth it is covered, and whether the subject of duty of care is included, is unknown.

The aim of this book is not to review coach training, discredit coach training providers who are providing robust training, or evaluate those who are not. Moreover, there is no empirical research data on the content of coach training programmes. Indeed, as 93% of training programmes attended by coaches were with an accredited/approved coaching organisation (ICF Global Coaching Study, 2020), drawing on the requirements for a programme to be accredited/approved leads to assumptions that ethics must have been included. However, as most coaches do not view their coach training as being formative in their sensemaking and understanding of ethics and duty of care (Mayhead, 2022), it begs the question of how ethics and duty of care feature in the formal learning and development of coaches. If you are reading this as a practitioner and are thinking of embarking on some coach training, I urge you to interrogate the programme content to ensure you are getting what you need regarding ethics training.

Codes of ethics and standards in coaching

Professional coaching membership bodies uphold ethical principles and best practices, and their codes of ethics provide guidance on standards, behaviours, and accountability for members. While not legally binding, the codes promote professional excellence, support development, and serve as a foundation for addressing complaints or other matters.

In coaching, reliance has been on the coaching bodies to set the standards and codes of ethics. Yet, whilst the codes of ethics might encompass duty of care, codes are not sufficiently clear nor explicit on meaning. One participant in my research remarked on how duty of care was 'baked in' to codes of ethics and how they considered it important that duty of care should be singled out and examined in its own right. Ethical codes go some way in providing coaches with frameworks on how to manage conflicts, conduct, integrity, contracting and other matters, yet the literature criticises coaching bodies for moving too far towards competence and skill bases (Bachkirova, 2017). Skills and competencies needed by coaches are stipulated by coaching bodies, but not all coaches are affiliated with or credentialled by such coaching bodies. Furthermore, skills and competencies alone do not suffice in educating coaches (Bachkirova and Smith, 2015). If we accept that coaches own their actions and are responsible for them, it must also be accepted that they have a responsibility and a duty of care for consequences and the impacts caused by their actions.

It is recognised that codes, frameworks, and guidelines do not remove the necessity for ethical awareness when determining how they should be applied in specific situations (Bond, 2015). Whilst it is acknowledged that codes cannot eliminate the need for ethical awareness, my research found that most coaches, regardless of whether they were a member of a coaching body, did not refer to codes of ethics when in a complex situation or ethical dilemma.

Research on the ethics of the coach most closely related to duty of care is limited, and previous studies have focused mainly on coaches who have affiliation with or membership of a coaching body and how they have used their codes of practice. Only one primary research study in the coaching literature shows how coaches make sense of ethical dilemmas (Diochon and Nizet, 2019). The study was focused on sensemaking during ethical dilemmas and included participants who were members of a coaching body. Throughout this book, reflections and accounts are shared from the voices of coaches who were members of a coaching body and those who weren't, along with their exploration of duty of care more broadly and not only during times of ethical dilemmas.

Literature on ethics in coaching emphasises that referring solely to codes when solving ethical dilemmas can be limiting and even dangerous (Louis and Fatien Diochon, 2019). Furthermore, codes may not be relevant to a particular situation or may be too simplistic or abstract and may present the coach with an obstacle (Louis and Fatien Diochon, 2019). Indeed, coaching bodies go some way towards providing ethical frameworks and codes, yet codes cannot fit all coaches, nor can they fit the multiple situations a coach will experience (Diochon and Nizet, 2015).

Duty of care is buried amongst frameworks and codes, while the focus in codes is primarily on a coach's competence and skill in relation to working with clients, professional conduct, and excellence in practice. Yet instruction in competence and skill fails to equip coaches for dealing with the

complexities and unpredictable challenges they face in real practice (Diochon and Nizet, 2015). Significantly, my own research found that all coaches,
without exception, saw duty of care as being vitally important. Yet, at the
time of publishing, coaching bodies do not cite duty of care explicitly in
their materials, with limited attention to legal and statutory obligations and
duties. Understandably, no single code of ethics can ever cover all legalities
across multiple common law jurisdictions. Therefore, we return again to the
coach's responsibility to ensure they seek, understand, and operate within
the law and statutory requirements of the common law jurisdiction they are
working in and develop an understanding of their own ethical obligations as
practitioners.

A further point to consider is that, as the growth of the coaching market is set to continue, and given the unregulated nature of coaching, there
is a risk that organisations could be exposed to incompetent or unethical
coaches (Schutte, 2019). Unregulated, the coaching industry is yet to have
standardised rules or one governing body to oversee practices. However,
even in regulated industries where strict rules and oversight exist, malprac-
tice still occurs. This highlights that while regulation can help reduce risk, it
cannot eliminate it entirely.

It is imperative that we examine duty of care, the legal and ethical dimensions, coaching standards, and codes of ethics as we have done, but we can't
afford to stop there. What we have discussed provides essential grounding,
but these elements do not exist in a vacuum. The landscape ahead is evolving
rapidly, shaped by the ever-shifting sands of AI and technological advance-
ments. The rise in digitally enabled tools, technology-informed coaching
platforms, algorithm-driven decision making, and the rising presence of AI
in coaching all introduce new complexities that demand our attention. As
practitioners, we must remain vigilant, continuously refining our awareness and reflexivity to ensure our ethical compass remains aligned amidst
these emerging changes. Let's now turn our attention to some of the issues
and opportunities offered by the shifting sands in technology and AI and the
challenges this brings for ethics and our duty of care as practitioners.

Shifting sands and the contemporary challenges of ethics with technology and AI

Technology and the fast evolution of AI represent a landscape that is continuously advancing, changing, and reshaping how we work and interact
with the world around us. The sands are shifting; time and again, these
topics are raised by coaches, mentors, and supervisors as one of the big-
gest contemporary challenges they face in how to stay ahead and adapt. In

this next section, attention is drawn to three areas – ethical considerations about our conduct in the virtual world we now find ourselves in, ethical implications for us with the rapid advancement of AI coaching in our field, and questions of ethics to consider when engaging with technology-enabled coaching platforms.

Organisations are increasingly turning to technology-enabled resources to gain competitive advantage; streamline and optimise operations; and enable the reach of coaching to many through the introduction of virtual, automated, or AI coaching. On making the decision to briefly include technology and AI in this chapter, I acknowledge the rapidity of development and change in this field and the acceptance that what follows will be superseded very quickly. That said, it would be remiss not to include a nod to the shifting sands of coaching and the contemporary challenges being experienced in relation to concerns of ethics and duty of care with AI and technology.

Our virtual world as practitioners

As a profession, like many others, we found ourselves thrown into a virtual world of working when the COVID-19 pandemic struck. My own research was conducted during this period, and Zoom enabled an opportunity for accessing a greater number of participants. There was ease in coordinating and conducting the interviews by video, with no travel involved. Furthermore, at that time, there were restrictions on movement and in-person contact. Using Zoom removed costs, reduced time needed, and enabled inclusion of participants from further afield. Clearly, the then-newly accessible virtual world of working continued long after the pandemic, and it has become almost a norm in how we practice, work, communicate, and conduct business.

With the rise of remote working and virtual communication, coaches, mentors, and coaching supervisors have responded and adapted to deliver services online, giving choice and flexibility to themselves and their clients. We are also seeing a shift, with some practitioners now working only online and not in person – a change from decades gone by. On the one hand, this allows greater access to more people and greater choice in which coach, mentor, or coach supervisor a client may choose to work with. Yet, on the other, this introduces a new mode of working and ethical considerations about our duty of care as practitioners.

Working online provides additional benefits outside of flexibility and choice. For example, recording coaching sessions enables greater visibility for the practitioners in their ongoing reflective practice and supervision with the supervisor, with the coach being able to watch or listen back to an entire session. The client can also refer back to and accurately recall points of action and interest from recordings (Berninger-Schäfer, 2022). However, this brings other ethical issues – for instance, how the session is being recorded. If through AI, it might be unknown where that data will be stored.

Until recently, ethics guidelines for working online have not been readily available for practitioners, with the coaching bodies now responding to the dynamic and rapid change being experienced. For the practitioner, addressing how they will be storing data and managing client information in the digital environment is crucial.

As practitioners, we have a responsibility to work ethically not only with managing client information and data storage but also considering where we conduct any virtual interactions. The coach has a responsibility to ensure they are in an area which is confidential, where the conversation cannot be overheard, and where client anonymity can be maintained. The same applies to the client, and whilst the coach can't control where the client takes virtual calls, the coach can include a discussion with the client and customer about confidentiality and avoiding interruptions at the contracting stage. Chapter 3 explores these areas further.

We must also consider how we approach ethical choices of video on or off and the client preference in this regard. Whether coaching sessions can be recorded (as was mentioned earlier) is another ethical decision which needs to be made, should the client ask for the session to be recorded, especially when automated AI text generators are to be used. Once recorded and/or transcribed, the coach cannot control how that data is used, nor can the client, if the other way round. The platform of choice, such as Teams or Zoom, must be considered, as some organisations do not permit calls conducted on Zoom due to security risks, for example. Being aware of these aspects and openly discussing with the client and customer can help ensure ethical practice and that choices are respected.

Ethical implications with the rapid advancement of AI coaching

The rapid advancement of AI has captivated the coaching community, sparking both excitement and apprehension (Bachkirova and Kemp, 2024). However, the same energy afforded to the excitement has not manifested in discussion and implications of ethics and duty of care. As a practitioner, I am yet to have confidence that these matters are being adequately addressed. This is an opportune time to invite and challenge those working in AI and technology, along with their supporters, to place ethics and duty of care at the forefront, ensuring these topics are approached with sufficient rigour and robustness. AI is causing disruption and transforming our field, and for us to properly compare human coaching with AI-driven coaching, we must first gain greater clarity on what it is that we do (Bachkirova, 2024).

Let's briefly take a look at the different types of coaching and where AI coaching may feature. On the one hand, goal attainment coaching can be helped with AI coaching, and it has been reported to the same level as human coaches (Terblanche, van Heerden and Hunt, 2024). On the other hand, coaches who work at a developmental level are perhaps less likely to be replaced by AI, as the capability of human intelligence and emotions is yet to be developed in AI coaching, although this development is fast progressing.

Studies into the efficacy of AI in coaching are limited (Terblanche, Molyn, De Haan and Nilsson, 2022). Research in related fields of psychology and healthcare domains has shown that AI can enhance wellbeing, build resilience, and reduce stress, and the AI systems used in these studies were specifically designed to integrate practices known to promote positive psychology outcomes (Terblanche et al., 2022). Leveraging techniques that focus on strengths, resilience, and cultivating a positive mindset can have demonstrated measurable impacts. Yet there are questions of ethics on how these AI systems ensure that harm is prevented. Questions arise regarding how to recognise and respond to individual vulnerabilities, avoid unintended distress, and guide users appropriately, especially when intervention from another profession, for instance in relation to mental wellbeing, may be required. The ethical implications surrounding accountability and safety remain significant.

Ethical concerns related to guidance on how AI is developed with ethics in mind; how clients are respected and autonomy maintained; and how data is used, stored, and managed have been raised. Terblanche et al. (2022) inform us that AI, simple in its nature, could be scaled to democratise coaching, used as a replacement for coaches who use model-based coaching, and we now see this happening. We have seen a rapid move to the advancement of products with AI 'cloning' technology, and this has spread to our domain of coaching, with practitioners being sold the possibility of scaling their businesses through developing 'clones' of themselves.

The European Artificial Intelligence Act, which came into force in August 2024, with most provisions applying from August 2026, is driving attention to standards. The Act represents the EU's first comprehensive legal framework to regulate AI technologies, aiming to ensure safety, transparency, and ethics standards across AI applications. Coaching bodies have responded through creating their own standards. For example, the ICF standards stress the importance of managing and safeguarding records associated with technology-assisted coaching. These records encompass all forms of documentation, including client session notes, audio or video files, and digital tool entries. Proper handling, storage and disposal of these must follow legal guidelines, such as the General Data Protection Regulation (GDPR), and ensure confidentiality through secure practices. Overall, the ICF standard underscores the need for vigilance in handling client data and maintaining ethical practices in the evolving technological landscape. This forms part of our duty of care.

Similarly, EMCC Global's guidelines emphasise the role technology and AI are playing in coaching, mentoring, and supervision, and stress the importance of maintaining professional conduct and enhancing the reputation of coaching, mentoring, and supervision services. EMCC states that coaches, mentors, and supervisors are expected to respect diverse practices within the profession, avoid any form of discrimination, and comply with legal and regulatory standards, particularly concerning data security. Furthermore, coaches, mentors, and supervisors should ensure that they are qualified, engage in ongoing professional development, and adhere to digital ethics, especially when using AI to deliver services. Overall, these guidelines aim to ensure ethical, superior, and responsible use of technology and AI in coaching, mentoring, and supervision.

Ethical considerations with technology-enabled coaching platforms

A further area related to this discussion is the fast development of technology-enabled coaching platforms which are entering the market. These are appealing commercially viable options for organisations to reach a wider audience with their coaching. A look at the market reveals an increasing number of these platforms emerging, some of which have both science advisory and commercial boards. Potential conflicts of interest are created when coaches are balancing goals and targets set by the coaching platform organisation with their own duty of care.

This tension arises when the coach prioritises meeting the imposed metrics or goals such as session quotas or a limited amount of time in between sessions over the unique needs and wellbeing of their clients. Such a focus risks turning the coaching relationship into a transactional one, where measurable results overshadow deeper issues such as mental health, emotional wellbeing, or personal development of the client. Additionally, the pressure to achieve targets may lead the coach to prioritise their own needs or the organisation's priorities rather than acting in the best interests of the client. This dynamic can undermine trust and erode the client's autonomy and poses questions of ethics. For coaches working in these domains, taking time to reflect and ensure ethical principles guide their actions is vital, even if this means questioning the goals set for them.

We have a responsibility as practitioners to be aware of the requirements and build in measures to ensure we are exercising our duty of care in relation to technology and AI uses. While we may find reassurance in the idea that technology and AI will not be replacing all of the human elements of our work, we are in a period of rapid change, and it's happening all around us – technology is increasingly integrating into our practices. Once again, it is our responsibility as individual practitioners to stay informed, to educate ourselves about these developments, and to form a robust understanding of the implications for our duty of care.

Implications for ethics and duty of care

As technology and AI become increasingly integrated into coaching, mentoring, and supervision, it introduces both opportunities and challenges related to our duty of care. AI tools are being used to analyse client data, provide insights, and offer personalised recommendations, amplifying the reach and efficiency of practitioners. AI 'cloning' of coaches as a practice is also being used, yet another way of increasing reach. However, these systems must be designed and used responsibly to avoid biases, breaches of confidentiality, or harm to clients. For practitioners, this means understanding the capabilities and limitations of AI tools, ensuring their ethical use, and supplementing them with human judgement and empathy.

The use of AI with 'cloning' coaches to the point where it becomes indistinguishable from a human coach raises ethical concerns, especially regarding the potential for clients to become secondary in the coaching process. While AI can offer efficiency and accessibility, there is a risk that the personalised, human-centred approach of traditional coaching may be diminished or lost. Coaches may prioritise profitability and scalability over the nuanced needs of individual clients, leading to a one-size-fits-all model that lacks the empathy, intuition, and understanding that human coaches can provide. We must also accept that AI 'cloned' coaches now replicating human interactions so closely further complicate matters, as clients may be unaware that they are not engaging with a human, potentially blurring the lines between genuine human support and artificial intelligence. This reliance on AI could contribute to the commodification of personal growth, thus reducing the depth and authenticity of the relationship between coach and client. In this context, the focus may shift toward the bottom line and commercial need rather than toward the genuine development, support, or wellbeing of the individual client.

To help practitioners navigate the complex intersection of AI and the human-centred practice of coaching, it's essential to expand the current conversation beyond the technical and operational aspects of AI implementation. While the integration of AI tools in coaching and other related fields offers immense potential, we cannot overlook the fundamental human element – the people these tools are designed to support.

It is our responsibility, as coaches, to recognise the profound impact that these technologies can have on clients and to act with a deep understanding of ethical considerations and our duty of care. AI tools can be used as instruments for efficiency, but we must consider the broader context where our duty of care to our clients takes precedence. We are working with real people, with complex needs, emotions, and aspirations. For myself as a practitioner, the technology should serve them, not replace the vital human connection that forms the heart of what we do as coaches.

It's crucial for us as practitioners to think critically before engaging with AI. Perhaps too often there is a rush to adopt new technologies without fully considering how they will affect the client who trusts us to act in their best interest. We need to pause and ask ourselves how these tools will enhance the work we do; how they will uphold the ethical standards we've committed to; and how they will respect the confidentiality, autonomy, and wellbeing of those we are working with.

Moreover, we need to understand that the responsibility of using AI ethically doesn't end with choosing the right tools. It extends throughout the entire process. From the moment we engage, we must be actively involved in ensuring its ethical alignment. We can do this by incorporating targeted training for practitioners, not only on how to evaluate and implement AI but also on how to assess potential impact on clients – an invitation here for more of this to be developed. The risks associated with mismanaging data or transparency can be profound. The even more subtle risk is the erosion of the client's trust.

To address this, suppliers and developers of AI tools can work in tandem with coaching professionals to develop systems that prioritise ethical conduct, client wellbeing, and clarity of purpose. We are seeing this happen in some areas, but as more platforms are launched, we run the risk of missing this part unless the suppliers and developers themselves are on board. Of course, as a minimum, this includes the ongoing implementation of regular audits to monitor the systems for alignment with evolving legal standards, data protection regulations, and the ethical guidelines to which we must hold ourselves accountable. Creating more spaces for meaningful collaboration between developers and coaching professionals is essential for ensuring these tools genuinely serve the needs of clients. Such collaboration can help bridge the gap between technology and human experience, ensuring that both systems and the practitioners using them can operate ethically, with the primary focus on the needs of the people we are committed to serving.

As practitioners, we bear the responsibility to think before we engage, to be aware of our duty of care and the potential consequences of adopting AI or technology enabled platforms, and to ensure that every decision we make upholds our commitment to those in the coaching relationship and to ethical practice. Asking questions of ourselves and thinking deeply about our 'digital coaching' environment can support our self-reflection (Buergi, Ashok and Clutterbuck, 2023). The tools we use should not overshadow the people we are here to support. Perhaps take a moment to reflect on what you think about this.

Concluding thoughts

Ethical codes aim to raise awareness and standards of practice across coaching bodies, and they also have a wider impact through helping shape and inform the work of those who may not be members but practice in the field. However, complete acceptance and reliance on the codes in isolation would be remiss. Coaches are encouraged to develop critical reflexivity in examining their own understanding of ethics and duty of care to cultivate a deeper awareness and personal interpretation of these concepts. Coaches rarely refer to their coaching body code of ethics in times of challenge or difficulty, or when in an ethical dilemma. Instead, the grey areas coaches experience in coaching assignments are discussed with peers or their coaching supervisor (Mayhead, 2022). Codes of ethics cannot cover every eventuality, and they cannot address the complexity and depth of duty of care.

Coaches need to develop their own sense and understanding of the implications for their own individual practice, both of their legal obligations in common law jurisdictions and ethical and moral considerations. Inroads have been made by coaching bodies through developing tools to assist with assessment and decision making in matters of ethics. These are complementary resources for codes of ethics and much needed in the development of coaching practice. However, we still have further to go in developing robustness in matters of practitioners' understanding of their legal and ethical responsibilities, including implications for their duty of care in relation to matters of technology and AI.

References

Bachkirova, T. (2017) 'Developing a knowledge base of coaching: Questions to explore'. https://radar.brookes.ac.uk/radar/items/f15792ac-73 0f-45f2-b087-22b819be6239/1/ https://doi.org/10.1037/0003-066X.46. 4.422

Bachkirova, T. (2024) 'Why coaching needs real intelligence, not artificial intelligence', *Philosophy of Coaching: An International Journal*, 9(2). https://dx.doi.org/10.22316/poc/09.2.02

Bachkirova, T. and Kemp, R. (2024) '"AI coaching": Democratising coaching service or offering an ersatz?', *Coaching: An International Journal of Theory, Research and Practice*, pp. 1–19. https://doi.org/10.1080/175218 82.2024.2368598

Bachkirova, T. and Smith, C. (2015) 'From competencies to capabilities in the assessment and accreditation of coaches', *International Journal of Evidence Based Coaching and Mentoring*, 13(2), pp. 123–140. https://doi. org/10.24384/IJEBCM

Berninger-Schäfer, E. (2022) 'The concept of online coaching', In *Online coaching*. Wiesbaden: Springer Fachmedien Wiesbaden. pp. 27–29. https:// doi.org/10.1007/978-3-658-39133-1_5

Bolam vs Friern Health Management Committee [1957] 1 W.L.R. 582 (QB).

Bond, T. (2015) *Standards and ethics for counselling in action*. 4th Ed. London: Sage. p. 306. *Book*. 2nd Ed. Thousand Oaks, CA: Sage.

Buergi, M., Ashok, M. and Clutterbuck, D. (2023) 'Ethics and the digital environment in coaching', In *The ethical coaches' handbook*. Routledge. pp. 369–381.

Carroll, M. and Shaw, E. (2013) *Ethical maturity in the helping professions: Making difficult life and work decisions*. UK: Jessica Kingsley Publishers.

Diochon, P.F. and Nizet, J. (2015) 'Ethical codes and executive coaches: One size does not fit all', *The Journal of Applied Behavioral Science*, 51(2), pp. 277–301. https://doi.org/10.1177/0021886315576190

Diochon, P.F. and Nizet, J. (2019) 'Ethics as a fabric: An emotional reflexive sensemaking process', *Business Ethics Quarterly*, 29(4), pp. 461–489. https://doi.org 10.1017/beq.2019.11

Garratt, D., Piper, H. and Taylor, B. (2013) 'Safeguarding' sports coaching: Foucault, genealogy and critique', *Sport, Education and Society*, 18(5), pp. 615–629. https://doi.org/10.1080/13573322.2012.736861

Hawkins, P. and Turner, E. (2019) *Systemic coaching: Delivering value beyond the individual*. UK: Routledge. https://doi.org/10.1037/1061-4087.55.2.94

ICF Global Coaching Study (2020) International Coaching Federation (ICF). https://coachingfederation.org/app/uploads/2020/09/FINAL_ICF_ GCS2020_ExecutiveSummary.pdf

Iordanou, I. (2018) 'What can we learn from sports and sports coaching', *Coaching: An International Journal of Theory, Research, and Practice*, 11(1), pp. 1–2. https://doi.org/10.1080/17521882.2018.1429194

Iordanou, I., Hawley, R. and Iordanou, C. (2017) *Values and ethics in coaching*. London: Sage. https://doi.org/10.4135/9781473983755

Louis, D. and Fatien Diochon, P. (2019) *Complex situations in coaching: A critical case-based approach*. Routledge. https://doi.org/10.4324/9780429056185

Lyle, J. (2019) 'What is ethical coaching?', *International Journal of Coaching Science*, 13(1).

Mayhead, B. (2022) 'Duty of care in coaching: From ethical frameworks to the development of the coach', Doctoral thesis. Oxford Brookes University. https://doi.org/10.24384/sjmq-9b67

Mitchels, B. and Bond, T. (2010) *Essential law for counsellors and psychotherapists*. London: Sage. https://doi.org/10.4135/9781446288818

Montgomery (Appellant v Lanarkshire Health Board (Respondent) Scotland)) (2015) UK Supreme Court. UKSC 1.

Partington, N. (2016) 'Modern sports coaching and the law: Analysing, clarifying and minimising negligence liability', Doctoral dissertation. Queen's University Belfast.

Partington, N. (2017) 'Sports coaching and the law of negligence: Implications for coaching practice', *Sports Coaching Review*, 6(1), pp. 36–56. https://doi.org/10.1080/21640629.2016.1180860

Partington, N. (2021) *Coaching, sport and the law: A duty of care*. New York: Routledge. https://doi.org/10.4324/9780429343148

Royal College of Nursing (2020) https://www.rcn.org.uk/get-help/rcn-advice/duty-of-care

Schutte, F. (2019) 'Business coaching: A hen with ducklings', *South African Journal of Business Management*, 50(1), pp. 1–7. https://doi.org/10.4102/sajbm.v50i1.398

Terblanche, N., Molyn, J., De Haan, E. and Nilsson, V.O. (2022) 'Coaching at scale: Investigating the efficacy of artificial intelligence coaching', *International Journal of Evidence Based Coaching & Mentoring*, 20(2). https://doi.org/10.24384/5cgf-ab69

Terblanche, N., van Heerden, M. and Hunt, R. (2024) 'The influence of an artificial intelligence chatbot coach assistant on human coach-client working alliance' *Coaching: An International Journal of Theory, Research and Practice*, 17(2), pp. 189–206. https://doi.org/10.1080/17521882.2024.2304792

Torda, A. (2005) 'How far does a doctor's "duty of care" go?', *Internal Medicine Journal*, 35(5), pp. 295–296. https://doi.org/10.1111/j.1445-5994.2005.00829.x

Williams, P. (2006) 'The profession of coaching. Law and ethics in coaching – how to solve and avoid difficult problems', In *Your practice*. Hoboken, NJ: John Wiley and Sons. pp. 3–20.

Wright, A. and O'Connor, S. (2021) 'Supervision for working legally', In *Coaching and mentoring supervision: Theory and practice*. 2nd Ed. UK: McGraw-Hill Education.

2 Building understanding of duty of care in coaching

Introduction

In Chapter 1, we discussed how we have drawn from related professional contexts to form our understanding of duty of care in coaching and how duty of care includes legal and ethical obligations. We also discussed how codes of ethics cannot cover all eventualities and how practitioners need to be aware of their responsibilities. Finally, we considered the shifting sands of technology and artificial intelligence, and the ethical challenges they present.

This next chapter first discusses the reasoning for introducing a definition of duty of care in coaching and presents vignettes from coaches illustrating what has shaped their understanding of duty of care. To protect the anonymity of the coaches who took part in the research, no names are used in these. Coaches acknowledge the significance of duty of care and its importance in their roles, yet few are able to clearly articulate what it means (Mayhead, 2022). A definition is shared, and the chapter concludes with an exercise designed to support further personal exploration.

Duty of care in coaching – to define or not to define?

As discussed in the Introduction, duty of care in coaching has not previously been defined. To define or not define duty of care in coaching is an interesting question, and there are positives and negatives for doing so. A definition could be a complementary resource for practitioners, as it could be helpful in ensuring we all have more of a common understanding of what duty of care means. The definition could also contribute to a stronger theoretical understanding of how duty of care is conceptualised. Importantly, a definition could be crucial for supporting ethical practice and setting clear expectations for all those in the coaching relationship. While existing research on duty of care in related helping professions sheds light on what it encompasses, there remains a lack of clarity on its specific meaning within the

DOI: 10.4324/9781003502494-3

coaching context. On the negative side, there are reasons a definition might not be appropriate or needed. A definition could portray the topic too simplistically, with meaning not explored. We must acknowledge that no single definition can possibly encompass all aspects and eventualities of the complexity of duty of care. We also know from related professions that duty of care is rarely defined, because of its complexity (Bond, 2015).

We have perhaps made assumptions about our understanding of duty of care in coaching, comfortable with and accepting the guidance of codes of ethics. We must keep the law in the forefront of our minds and be aware of our legal obligations in the common law jurisdictions in which we work. In the Introduction, attention was drawn to cultural difference and how each situation is unique, and coaches must be aware of obligations in each common law jurisdiction in which they practice.

Coaches draw on their own past experiences when making sense of what duty of care means to them and how they enact it. We know enactment includes managing boundaries, contracting, and ending coaching relationships (Mayhead, 2022). Coaches draw on influence from role models and from their own life experience, but less so from textbooks or codes of ethics when making sense of what duty of care means to them (Mayhead, 2022). We must also consider the implications of projecting our own past experiences onto new situations and how this might not be ethically sound and could be problematic. Coaching is complex, with ethical practice central to a coach's work. The coach sets and maintains the limits and boundaries, executed in part through contracting and re-contracting. In my research, coaches expressed all of these elements as ways in which they enacted their duty of care (Mayhead, 2022).

Whilst related psychology-based professions of psychotherapy and counselling have helped inform our understanding of duty of care, borrowing from helping professions might suggest underlying assumptions about the nature and context of helping relationships, often introducing concepts and tools that are unsuitable for the organisational settings of coaching (Fatien Diochon, Louis and Islam, 2022). In contrast, coaching operates on the core assumption that clients are inherently resourceful, which has significant implications for distinguishing it from counselling or therapy, where such a default assumption about client agency or resourcefulness may not be typically made. This distinction shapes the approaches and practices within coaching, such as the coach's neutrality, often adopted to maintain a facilitative and non-judgemental relationship with the client. But this default position still lacks theorisation (Fatien Diochon et al., 2022).

In addition to the challenges of incorporating psychology-based ideas and practices into coaching, the field has faced divergent opinions about aspects of coaching philosophy and the difficulties organisations face in adopting socially embedded responsibilities (Fatien Diochon et al., 2022). Organisations are increasingly challenged to embrace broader social responsibilities, with the argument that coaching has the potential to contribute to societal wellbeing on a global scale (Boyatzis, Hullinger, Ehasz, Harvey, Tassarotti, Gallotti and Penafort, 2022). This challenge was explored in collaboration with the International Coaching Federation (ICF), with the aim of delivering positive outcomes by sharing knowledge that aligns coaching with the United Nations Action Plan for societal wellbeing for individuals, organisations, and communities (UN General Assembly, 2015). However, this work also highlighted a potential risk: any activity that appears to help people, including coaching, can lead to that activity outrunning itself and away from its research-based intellectual foundations (Boyatzis et al., 2022).

Introducing a definition for duty of care in coaching gives an opportunity to pause and slow down the outrunning. A definition can help guide practice for greater clarity on shared understanding. Grounding the definition in empirical research and literature from related professional contexts ensures it is informed by and aligns with established principles. Before we get to a definition, however, let us first explore what we know about how coaches make sense of duty of care. Their sensemaking is phenomenologically informed from their experiences, role models and lives, and own development. The vignettes shared in this next section are from my research, presenting personal accounts from practitioners.

Making sense of duty of care

Coaches' experiences

Experiences shared by coaches about what has informed their sensemaking of duty of care follow from here. We know from research that coaches make sense of their own duty of care primarily through reflections on their own life experiences, their values and beliefs, and their growth and development in coaching, while codes of ethics or textbooks on best practice are not central to their sensemaking (Mayhead, 2022). Instead, coaches' understanding of duty of care is shaped from a variety of factors. For example, role models and experiences influence coaches' own philosophies of life, which in turn inform what duty of care means to them. This is a continually shaping process, with supervision and reflective dialogue with peers and colleagues playing a significant role and giving the coach greater depth of understanding beyond the words that form a code of ethics (Mayhead, 2022).

Lived experiences from childhood, family members, teachers, life experiences, values, and a sense of one's own humanity are some of the main factors that shape the meaning of duty of care for coaches (Mayhead, 2022). Coaches describe unique role models who embodied duty of care through integrity, responsibility, and respect. One coach described how duty of care came from his humanity and from what he'd learned from his parents. In another case, acknowledgement was given to a traumatic life experience from which the coach drew strength and compassion, and this informed how they viewed their own practice as a coach. Another coach described how family members and teachers had helped shape his values as a person and how he operated now as a coach. He described how his sense of duty of care had grown stronger with age, with his values of kindness and caring developing further.

Each coach has their own experience and unique life story. We know that developing ethical maturity is one element in how a coach can further develop understanding of themselves and how they align their personal values and beliefs through congruent expression of their coaching approach (Bachkirova, 2016). Developing ethical maturity includes having sensitivity, drawing on one's own values to help guide moral decisions of right and wrong. Ethical sensitivity can be expressed through the compassion, empathy, and care a practitioner brings to their work. This development is an ongoing and complex process, with coaches continuously integrating their backgrounds, experiences, and evolution of self-understanding. Ethical maturity and self-awareness help shape how coaches navigate their practice, influencing the actions and approaches to be in alignment with their values. Indeed, ethics are a practical application of values, with values and attitudes sitting hand in hand (Iordanou, Hawley and Iordanou, 2017).

To help illustrate how coaches make sense of duty of care, let us explore accounts from coaches about how they have shaped and informed their own understanding of it – their lived experiences. For most coaches interviewed in my research, it was the first time they had deeply thought about what duty of care meant to them. Wrangling with making sense of the concept was a common experience during the interviews, and for some, duty of care was hiding in plain sight, as one coach explained:

> *I think I can, and I do know I care for my clients, and I think I'm really, really good at caring for them, but I'd never thought of the concept of duty of care, if I'm honest, and that now you've raised, it is so obvious.*

Not uncommon for coaches was the experience that this was the first time they had stopped to articulate where meaning of duty of care came from for them. But when they did, what emerged was truly fascinating for them, a phenomenological perspective, an area of themselves they had not previously thought about. Coaches said the process of reflecting in the moment and thinking deeply about what had formed their understanding of duty of care was hugely developmental and helpful. As you are reading, I invite you to take the opportunity to reflect on what it means to you.

Role models and life

From a moral and ethical perspective, coaches' perceptions of duty of care are shaped by a variety of factors. Role models and life experiences influence coaches' own philosophies of life, which in turn inform their own meaning of duty of care. This is a continually shaping process, with supervision and reflective dialogue playing significant roles – as shall be discussed later in this book – giving greater depth beyond the words that form an ethical code of practice or indeed the law (Mayhead, 2022).

Parents, family members, teachers, life experiences, and a sense of one's own humanity are the main factors that shape the moral and ethical sense of duty of care (Mayhead, 2022). One coach shared how unique role models who represented duty of care 'embodied integrity and responsibility and respect'. Another coach shared how 'duty of care comes from my humanity, and it comes from my parents and what I've learned along the way'. In another case, acknowledgement was given to a traumatic life experience from which the coach drew strength and compassion, which I share with you here:

> I think I'd like to give credit to my upbringing. I've seen that [duty of care] from very close quarters, ever since I was 10 years old. I lost my mum when I was two, two and a half, but I don't remember much of that, but I lost my grandparents [who raised her when her mother passed], one when I was 10 and the second one, when I was going on to being 12, . . . and my grandparents role modelled it [duty of care] in their giving themselves in caring, tending to the needs of my father who was much younger than them, when it should have been the other way around. They were around to nurture us, nourish us, you know, look after us and be the support for my father. I also picked it up from some other friends of mine, especially this friend who lost everything in an unfortunate incident, but she was still willing to share everything that remained with her in terms of belongings. She lost all her family members in an accident – unfortunately they were all travelling together, so after that, the way she came out and supported people by giving away

> belongings, not only of those who departed but those who are with her, and her own stuff. She moved from a luxury life to a minimalistic life by choice. All these and many other incidents in my life, including my in-laws. I got married very early so seeing them give themselves to serving others, my father-in-law especially you know, he was always talking about serving people, so I think I picked up empathy, being there for the others. He was always coming from a place of obligation to ensure the safety and wellbeing with anyone he came in touch with. So, I've experienced this, not as an obligation but as an opportunity with those I interact with.

This coach considered they had an 'opportunity', not an 'obligation', to be there for others, and this informed how they enacted their duty of care in coaching. Their words of tending to the needs of others, nurturing and nourishing, supporting, willingness, serving, empathy, and being there for others all relate to what duty of care meant to them. Yet over-helping and rescuing are also shadow elements which might have crept in. Role models featured in accounts from many coaches, with another coach sharing where their shaping of duty of care came from:

> Certainly, it came from my dad who was an extremely upright, a thoughtful man. He used to agonise over his misdemeanours as well. So, he cared a lot about how he conducted himself, and I think that he was the model my mother, oddly enough, was not. She was a complete wildcat, and you know, I didn't get any moral compass from her identity. I can't deny that school was important. We had a great headmaster, and he was another role model, I think. So, it's actually coming down to role models. I have an important aunt as well, who had quite a profound influence on me – she was a lifelong buddy and so it was probably from role models, I would say, and from exploring with them, you know. And my aunt, particularly, I could talk to her about anything. And she wasn't moralistic at all, so you never felt as though you were being preached at, but she would listen and sometimes she would tell me stuff.

Family members and a teacher helped this coach make sense of duty of care: those who listened and were open-minded with being able to talk about anything and those who were aware of how they conducted themselves – her father in this case. The presence of positive role models can guide our process, while the ability to explore ethical questions without judgement, as facilitated here by her aunt, helps deepen the understanding of what our duty of care is to others. For others, however, their sense of duty of care came more from within, with a natural development of compassion and kindness growing and developing as they became older in adult life:

> *My own sense [of duty of care] has got stronger as I've got older, com-*
> *passion and kindness and caring about the individual and individual*
> *working, caring about an individual is just naturally something I've*
> *always done, and I say that deliberately, an individual rather than an*
> *organisation or something bigger, and I don't think that comes from my*
> *parents. Sometimes I think they aren't as thoughtful and caring about*
> *other people, I see things sometimes they do, and I just think gosh that*
> *really surprises me, I wouldn't do that. So, I think that's always been*
> *there in me, but I think maybe that's why I'm drawn to the work [coach-*
> *ing], I'm sure.*

Experiences from childhood, family and life, philosophy of life, and values inform how coaches make sense of duty of care. Philosophy of life was expressed in different ways, from showing kindness and compassion to having choices:

> *I think it's [duty of care] about philosophy and values, . . . I think it*
> *comes back to what your philosophy of life is, you know. So, my philoso-*
> *phy of life is you've got endless choices, you can do anything that you*
> *want to do, you're capable of doing great things. Try to figure out what*
> *it is you want to do, and then, I am just there to nudge.*

The coach here considered their duty of care included nudging the client further towards where the client chose to be, thus working to the client's needs. Having an influence or nudging others involves understanding the ripple effect and potential impact a coach has on others (later in the book we will explore duty of care from a systemic perspective and consider this ripple effect). Therefore, being mindful of how a coach engages is important. Yet, we are not static, and one interaction is not the same as the next. Another coach expressed this by way of sharing their thinking on how we show up in the world:

> *I do believe that we evolve and change, and every interaction that we*
> *have in the world has some kind of ripple effect. Which means we need*
> *to be mindful about how we engage and show up in the world, and so*
> *that's I guess a long-winded way of saying this is evolved from a level of*
> *law, from a duty of care as a legal construct, to this overarching concept*
> *of being in the world.*

Coaches saw there was a ripple effect to interactions they had, with duty of care ever changing and evolving, itself being part of the ripple. It was evident from the research that duty of care had multiple meanings for coaches, yet fundamentally their sensemaking of what is right and wrong came from their values, beliefs, philosophy of life, experiences and role models (Mayhead, 2022). These points very much relate to the coach as a whole person, not just in their professional role. Who we are as a person and who we are as a coach are inextricably linked. Our values and beliefs traverse our roles outside of our work and as coaches. As with life experiences, our own development as coaches also shapes us.

Coach development

For coaches, understanding and perception of duty of care is continually developing, with new perspectives and awareness shaped through new experiences and situations. As one coach explained:

> *I think everything we do changes us, as coaches. Whatever happens adds a new value to our competencies as coaches, whether it's success, whether it's a dilemma, whether it's hesitancy, I think everything, every experience with a new client or with the same client adds a new experience to your competency. Does it change you? I think it does bring awareness. It does bring new perspectives and new ways of seeing things and understanding others.*

The sense of duty of care is continually evolving. What has gone before remains with us and what is added enriches what is there. The richness and depth of understanding of our duty of care is developed through the continual shaping of experience and learning, leading to greater complexity which in turn requires care and attention for the coach in how they see more than they have previously seen (Mayhead, 2022). Coaching supervision plays a vital part in this development, as duty of care becomes more complex, as illustrated in this coach's reflection:

> *Supervision helps us see more than we could previously see, see more in ourselves, more in others, more in the systems in which we operate, and so I think it helps us recognise legal challenges and ethical challenges when perhaps we might not always see them – it helps us navigate them.*

Supervision plays an important role with coaches in how they assess and avoid doing harm and being very clear about it with themselves (we shall explore supervision in greater detail later in the book). It forms part of a coach's development and growth. Having an environment where supervision is central to that exploration is key, as another coach shared:

> I think that's why supervision is such an important piece for us. There is a real sense of, you know, professionalism and, do no harm. The environment I am in is very conscious and aware [of duty of care], even if we don't express it in language; . . . an environment where duty of care is central to a coach's practice, even if not expressed in language.

For this coach, working in a practice where supervision was centrally important to them, and part of the culture of how they operated was really beneficial. There is a layer of complexity around coaches and emergent coaches who are new to the field, and supervision can help them get uncomfortably comfortable with self-revealing within the supervision context, able to work through the doing no harm part, and reflect on duty of care.

Coaches also talked of emotional and psychological burdens, which at times had a lasting impact on them. Coaches can experience immense worry for their clients, and at times they have to work hard to push clients from their minds. They experience how some clients stay metaphorically with them long after coaching assignments have ended, and supervision offers a space to explore this. One coach described this as a boundary point:

> There's also that boundary point about where you can't just spend your life worrying about what other people are up to after your sessions, so you just have to cut off a bit and make sure you don't over commit. There's definitely a duty of care to myself, and I think there's a lot of learning in what you do for yourself, you learn from your own experience.

Role modelling healthy boundaries with how to 'cut off' as a coach and not worrying about what is happening outside of coaching sessions is more achievable when working with less complex coaching assignments. However, more serious matters, such as suicide risk and mental health implications, can lead to coaches finding themselves in assignments where they have deep concern and worry for a client's wellbeing.

Experiences of anxiety and worry may manifest into a compelling need for the coach to take action. Along with empathy and compassion, the coach moves to the position of how to remain objective, how to ascertain what their responsibility is in a given situation, and how to determine the legal position. Finally, the coach makes decisions on what to do. Whilst fearing risk of suicide of a client may seem a rarity, research has found multiple accounts from coaches having been in this or similar situations, where the coach made the decision to enact their duty of care by signposting the client, by having clear escalation procedures in their contracts of engagement, or by asking for an emergency contact in private coaching engagements (Mayhead, 2022).

Defining duty of care in coaching

By way of introducing a definition, I add an important note of caution to accompany it. The definition is not offered to be pinned up in a reception area nor on a website to say 'this is our duty of care'. As one participant in my research said, 'if we can write what duty of care means neatly in one sentence, we've missed the point completely'. Instead, the definition is intended to be a richer offering and to act as a developmental tool for coaches and supervisors alike. I extend the invitation to you to take the definition and explore and interrogate it, with the aim of helping inform and shape your own ethical practice.

> *Duty of care is an ethical and legal obligation for the coach not to cause harm and forms part of the ethical framework of conduct encompassing the coach's adherence to a standard of reasonable professional care. The coach's responsibility includes setting and maintaining boundaries between ethically acceptable and unacceptable influence on the client, customer, and those in the coaching relationship.*

Let's explore the definition further. It highlights the ethical and legal obligations of the coach and draws attention to how the coach must not cause harm. Those who are in the coaching relationship will vary, dependent on the context, and the element of proximity requires consideration. The context might include the coach, the client the coach is coaching, and the client's organisation – the customer. It might include only the coach and client, or there may be an associate organisation the coach is working for, and it may include others. The coach needs to assess carefully who the parties are and to act accordingly.

The definition foregrounds how the coach is expected to set and maintain the boundaries to the work they are conducting in relation to those in the coaching relationship. The coach is responsible for assessing what is ethically acceptable and unacceptable influence and to act accordingly. Enactment of their duty of care involves setting expectations through contracting, re-contracting, and endings of coaching engagements.

In the following chapters we will explore boundaries and standards, the art of contracting, how we develop a duty to care, endings in coaching relationships, how adopting a systemic lens can help us, and the role supervision plays. All of these form part of our enactment of duty of care, bringing the definition off the page and into life and encouraging us to question and think critically about our actions.

Concluding thoughts

This chapter ends with an exercise which allows you to think about the concepts discussed. We know from research that coaches' sensemaking on what duty of care means to them comes from their life experience, role models, and own development (Mayhead, 2022). Chapter 1 discussed how coaching has drawn from other related professional contexts to form our codes of ethics and current understanding, with coach development being a continual cycle. A definition for duty of care in coaching was offered in this chapter, accompanied by a note of caution – it is a tool for us to help inform and shape our own ethical practice. With that in mind, the following exercise invites you to reflect on a series of questions built from the definition.

Your practice in focus

Let's now use the definition as a reflection point to explore our understanding. The wording in the definition has been developed into an exercise as follows. Either alone or with someone else (such as a fellow coach, peer, colleague, coach supervisor, coach trainer or educator, or network group), use the exercise to challenge your own understanding and thinking.

Reflect on and answer the following questions, providing examples where you can. Think about where your own values have come from, what has shaped your beliefs around ethical issues, and how this shows up for you today. Consider also what ethical beliefs you might be projecting onto your clients and what risks there are with this.

Reflection 1 – *Duty of care is an ethical and legal obligation for the coach not to cause harm.*

What does an ethical obligation mean to you?

What are your legal obligations?

What examples do you have of when a coach could cause harm?

Reflection 2 – *Duty of care forms part of the ethical framework of conduct encompassing the coach's adherence to a standard of reasonable professional care.*

What standards do you adhere to?

If you are a member of a coaching association, how do these standards differ dependent on your level of accreditation/credentials? For example, if you are a Master Coach with the EMCC or ICF, what difference is there in what the client can expect compared to the standard of an Associate Coach?

What does reasonable care mean to you?

What are the implications for providing too much care or not enough?

What ethical framework of conduct do you follow? This might be from your coaching association, but if you are not a member of a coaching association, perhaps take this opportunity to refer to the Global Code of Ethics.

Critically review the codes and evaluate how they apply to you and your practice.

Reflection 3 – *The coach's responsibility includes setting and maintaining boundaries between ethically acceptable and unacceptable influence on the client, customer, and those in the coaching relationship.*

How do you enact your duty of care?

How do you establish and maintain the boundaries in your coaching practice?

What would you be doing if you were exercising ethically acceptable influence?

What would you be doing if you were exercising unacceptable influence?

Reflection 4 – *Moving forward.*

After reflecting on and answering these questions, what do you notice about your practice?

What changes would you like to make?

What would help you achieve that change?

How will you articulate your duty of care to those you work with?

What steps will you take to ensure all those in the coaching relationship have clarity?

How did you find this exercise? What did you notice about yourself?

These questions are a helpful developmental tool for us to return to at regular intervals. You may choose to come back to them after having read more of the book. When working with clients, consider how you can articulate to them what your duty of care is and how you will demonstrate it to them. A coach who has a deeper understanding of their practice is better placed within the ethical and legal parameters, reducing risk of straying beyond the accepted boundaries of their work.

References

Bachkirova, T. (2016) 'The self of the coach: Conceptualization, issues, and opportunities for practitioner development', *Consulting Psychology Journal: Practice and Research*, 68(2), pp. 143–156. https://doi.org/10.1037/cpb0000055

Bond, T. (2015) *Standards and ethics for counselling in action*. 4th Ed. London: Sage. p. 306. *Book*. 2nd Ed. Thousand Oaks, CA: Sage.

Boyatzis, R., Hullinger, A., Ehasz, S., Harvey, J., Tassarotti, S., Gallotti, A. and Penafort, F. (2022) 'The grand challenge for research on the future of coaching', *The Journal of Applied Behavioral Science*, 58(2), pp. 202–222. https://doi.org/10.1177/00218863221079937

Fatien Diochon, P.F., Louis, D. and Islam, G. (2022) 'Neutral in-tensions: Navigating neutrality in coaching', *Journal of Management Studies*. https://doi.org/10.1111/joms.12883

Iordanou, I., Hawley, R. and Iordanou, C. (2017) *Values and ethics in coaching*. London: Sage. https://doi.org/10.4135/9781473983755

Mayhead, B. (2022) 'Duty of care in coaching: From ethical frameworks to the development of the coach', Doctoral thesis. Oxford Brookes University. https://doi.org/10.24384/sjmq-9b67

United Nations General Assembly (2015) *Resolution adopted by the general assembly on 25 September, 2015: Transforming our world: The 2030 agenda for sustainable development*. United Nations.

3 Boundaries and standards in coaching

Introduction

In this chapter we will examine how part of a coach's fulfilment and application of duty of care includes setting and maintaining boundaries, and we will explore the meaning of standards for the coach. In the first two chapters, we have discussed the multiple facets of legal and ethical considerations surrounding duty of care in coaching. This chapter concludes with a discussion of the importance of the coach's self-awareness – coaches must first understand themselves and their own capabilities.

'What is my responsibility as the coach?' This was a question brought to supervision recently by a newly qualified coach grappling with the question of who takes the lead in the delicate and transformative dance of coaching. Whilst coaching can include the coach, the client(s), and the customer, and assuming all parties are adults, the question of where responsibility lies in coaching arises often in supervision sessions.

Setting the scene

Let's consider agency in the context of the coach/client relationship, a notion rooted in self-efficacy, where the individual (the client in this case) is proactively engaged in their development and where their own actions make things happen. Agency is a potential, available at all times but not always exercised (Lefstein, Vedder-Weiss, Tabak and Segal, 2018). Exercising agency depends on multiple factors, including a person's disposition, their ability, and how they identify with and see themselves (Lefstein et al., 2018). When we enter into a coaching assignment, from my experience as coach, we do not, nor should we, control the outcomes for the client. We can support in creating the right environment for learning and manage the process with clear agreements, boundaries, and standards, but the client

DOI: 10.4324/9781003502494-4

owns their actions. We can help the client exercise agency, but ultimately, it is down to them.

The coach shares a privileged position with their clients, and this relationship goes beyond the standards of professional ethics and into the realms of absolute confidentiality and high trust. However, our world of coaching is far less organised than those of other mature professions such as law or the world of medicine, and whilst we have our codes of ethics and standards, these cannot suffice in guiding us as practitioners through the complexity of our work.

It is for the coach to set and maintain the boundaries and to take an active role in upholding, protecting, and maintaining the standards. The coach ensures the coaching follows an agreed-upon structure related to how many sessions and at what intervals and moving with the client's needs. The coach strives to ensure the boundaries are ethical and clear and are kept within the scope of coaching, and the coach upholds ethical and professional standards, guided in part by codes of ethics.

The ethical maturity of the coach is a continual, complex cycle, with coaches bringing their own backgrounds, experience, and values into their development, as we explored earlier in the book. Being responsible for setting and maintaining the boundaries and standards requires coaches to operate ethically within the boundaries of their own skill and own level of experience. This requires them to assess what is ethically acceptable and unacceptable influence and how to act accordingly.

Agreement of services

Contract law is the body of law that is concerned with the rights and obligations of those parties under an agreement. It governs the relationship, the validity, and the interpretation of the agreement made, be that the sale of goods, the provision of services (such as coaching or coaching supervision), or the exchange of interests of ownership. Three elements are needed for a contract to be legally binding – an agreement, an intention to form a legally binding relationship, and consideration (or payment). Having written agreement of services can help with setting and maintaining boundaries and standards, although agreements can also be verbal.

Agreement of services may differ, dependent on the parties involved in the coaching relationship. Helpful to have, they define the expectation, responsibilities, and boundaries between the coach, the client, and the customer, where relevant, ensuring a professional and transparent relationship. Coaches, clients, and the customer could all be exposed should they enter into coaching without a clear understanding of what has been agreed.

By ensuring attention is paid to this matter and ensuring agreements are in place, coaches can tighten their practice areas, thus demonstrating their duty of care to their clients and customers, as well as to themselves. This serves as a protection for all parties. For those coaches who are members of a coaching body, standard templates for agreements are available for use, yet it is advisable to seek independent professional advice when entering into complex agreements or if in any doubt about the suitability of an agreement.

Key points in an agreement include detailing who the parties in the coaching engagement are, such as the coach as the service provider or supplier and the client or customer (that being an individual or an organisation) as the recipient. The agreed-upon duration, such as commencement and term of the contract, the services to be provided, and how these will be delivered with reasonable care and skill and in accordance with relevant law and regulations, can be included. The coach may also specify adherence to a code of ethics, such as the Global Code of Ethics or a relevant coaching body's guidelines.

Health and safety security protocols should be addressed, especially when a coach is working at their clients' premises. Also included will be management of the client's materials and data, and compliance with GDPR and other relevant data protection laws. How personal data will be handled and outlining measures in place to protect against unauthorised processing or accidental loss can also be included.

Confidentiality is another important aspect, and the agreement may include how both parties agree not to disclose any confidential information related to the business, the clients, or employees or suppliers, except as required by law. Payment terms and charges, including fees, should be clearly stated, in addition to any limitations of liability and details of the coach's insurance in respect of their own legal liability such as professional indemnity and public liability insurance.

These points do not cover everything that might be included but are suggested as a necessary foundation to ensure clarity and mutual understanding, serving as protection for all parties involved. Furthermore, this applies regardless of whether the coaching is being charged for. If a coach is working pro bono, not charging fees for a service, as can often be the case when a coach is starting to build their practice and gain experience, the need to have agreements in place still applies.

Boundaries

We know from the first part of this book how our duty of care as practitioners resides within the ethical framework of conduct regarding how an individual acts (Brennan and Wildflower, 2018). Five themes are evident in ethical frameworks created for professional contexts related to coaching: 1) do no harm, 2) duty of care, 3) know your limits, 4) respect the interests of the client, and 5) respect the law (Brennan and Wildflower, 2018).

From my own experience as a coaching supervisor, many ethical dilemmas brought by coaches to supervision involve the topic of boundaries and how to manage them. Yet research confirms that efforts made to establish clear boundaries between coaching and therapy, for example, have been unhelpful to both fields, as the primary distinctions are artificially constructed and tend to be less distinct in actual practice (Kitchin, 2024). We have a responsibility as practitioners, therefore, to explore boundary management and appreciate how it forms part of how we enact our duty of care.

Before delving into the 'how to' part of this section, let's first consider what we mean by boundaries, drawing from the related profession of counselling. The British Association for Counselling and Psychotherapy defines boundaries as the foundation for the therapeutic relationship, providing a structured environment for the work to take place. Boundaries are complex in nature and encompass both practical and interpersonal elements. The practical aspects include, amongst other elements, the working space, the length of sessions, fees, confidentiality, contact between sessions, social media policy, and the duration or number of sessions. The interpersonal elements include dual relationships, self-disclosure, physical contact, non-professional interactions, and, importantly, practitioner competence. By clearly defining the purpose of the relationship and outlining what clients can expect, clear boundaries can help clients feel secure and can help build trust.

We know from the literature that the situations coaches face are complex and unique, such as the presence of multiple agendas, power issues, and boundary challenges (Louis and Fatien Diochon, 2014, 2019). Extant literature on boundaries in coaching gives guidance to coaches on how to identify boundaries and how to manage them (Lancer, Clutterbuck and Megginson, 2016). Best practice is argued as including, amongst other points, contracting and re-contracting, helping the client not to depend on the coach, and when to refer a client (Lancer et al., 2016).

Further interrogation of the literature provides sources of support for coaches in understanding the boundaries between coaching and counselling (Bachkirova and Baker, 2018), often a complex area for coaches to navigate and an issue for coaches in understanding where their duty of care lies. Bachkirova and Baker (2018) go some way towards helping coaches differentiate between coaching and counselling through a review of literature which has explored the views of coach practitioners. Coaching, counselling, and psychotherapy are described as often being 'artificially separated'. It is not as straightforward as separating them by suggesting coaching deals with the present and future, and counselling and psychotherapy deal with the past (Popovic and Boniwell, 2007). There are grey areas when the lines of separation are blurred.

Authors have discussed boundaries in the coaching process, internal boundaries of the client, boundaries of the coaching relationship, and boundaries in organisational systemic perspectives (Farr and Shepheard, 2018; Roberts and Brunning, 2018; Lawrence, 2021; Wilson, 2019). Western (2012) describes coaching as being a contested 'field' with 'fuzzy' boundaries and multiple identities, pointing to its nebulous nature and complexity. So, with multiple definitions of boundaries, it is unsurprising that we can experience difficulty in exactly pinpointing the boundaries in the context of coaching.

A review of literature from a broader context draws attention to organisational management consultancy, which has developed its conversation on boundaries and knowledge flow in relation to physical, cultural, and political boundaries (Sturdy, Clark, Fincham and Handley, 2009). Let's look at other fields: in nursing, a boundary is described as the edge of what would be considered suitable or professional behaviour, and crossing it would mean the therapist is no longer acting within their clinical role (Gutheil and Simon, 2002). In sports coaching, boundaries are often permeable and are concerned with what appropriate and workable boundaries are for the coach when factors can affect the performance, and the enjoyment, of the athlete (Cassidy, Jones and Potrac, 2015).

Coming back to related helping professions, in counselling and the talking therapies, boundaries are succinctly defined as follows: 'boundaries: set the limits between ethically acceptable and unacceptable influence over others or the line between acceptable and unacceptable relationships' (Bond, 2015, p. 305). Let us explore this definition and its meaning and apply it to coaching and what it means when we consider our duty of care.

The first element in Bond's (2015) definition of 'setting the limits' is owned by the coach. The literature discusses this point in relation to the professional boundaries of the coach's role and how this can be laid out at the contracting stage of a coaching engagement (Iordanou, Hawley and Iordanou, 2017). For the coach, a clear understanding between themselves and their client/customer on their engagement, and the boundaries of that engagement, is required. The coach must further consciously consider their actions and judge what is prudently expected. This is typically addressed in the contracting stages of coaching (Lee, 2013; Gettman, Edinger and Wouters, 2019).

We will explore in detail the art of contracting in the next chapter, but briefly and for context now, contracting within a coaching relationship is acknowledged as a way to reduce various ethical challenges that may arise (Iordanou et al., 2017). Contracting is not only concerned with the legal side of having a contract or agreement of services but is also concerned with the subtleties of expectation on the part of the client, the organisation, and the coach, such as matters relating to confidentiality (Iordanou et al., 2017). However, as coaching engagements are live situations, dynamic in nature, with multiple moving parts, contracting is arguably a process point that coaches must re-visit and engage with through re-contracting, yet empirical research on this aspect is not evidenced in coaching literature.

Coaches consider contracting and re-contracting part of their enactment of their duty of care, and they often do so regularly, even with multiple occurrences of re-contracting within one coaching session (Mayhead, 2022). Contracting and re-contracting are a central part of the coach's application of their duty of care in relation to maintaining and managing boundaries and not just when an organisation is involved (Mayhead, 2022; Louis and Fatien Diochon, 2019). Furthermore, contracting at the start of coaching and re-contracting also include contracting for ending engagements (we will explore endings in Chapter 6), an additional part of how the coach enacts their duty of care (Mayhead, 2022).

A further element relating to contracting concerns the boundaries of access to a coach, a coach's duty of care in relation to the access the client has to them, and their availability to the client. Boundaries of access to the coach differ from coach to coach, and part of contracting is concerned with setting the boundaries in relation to the limits of the coaching engagement (Bond, 2015; Iordanou et al., 2017; Far and Shepheard, 2018), which includes access. For some coaches, being available 24 hours every day through text messaging or WhatsApp is the norm, whereas other coaches might only correspond through email and during office hours (we'll explore this in more detail in the next chapter). What must be considered is for whose benefit access is permitted, and to what impact on all parties.

Standards

In the context of coaching, it is important we understand what is meant by standards. Standards establish the expected level of competence and ethical responsibilities coaches must uphold to ensure the wellbeing of all those in the coaching relationship. In legal terms, a 'standard' is the level of caution or diligence that a practitioner is expected to exercise to prevent harm or damage to others and that is determined by the behaviour of a reasonable person in a similar situation.

In coaching, the 'standard of reasonable care' also relates to the level at which a coach positions himself or herself. The coaching bodies have various levels of accreditation or credentialling. For example, the ICF has three levels – Associate Certified Coach, Professional Certified Coach, and Master Certified Coach. A coach who is credentialled as a Master Certified Coach has a duty to deliver a standard to that level, different to that of an Associate Certified Coach. The requirements for membership at these levels may be clear for the coach, yet what the client or customer can expect from each coach at the different levels is not typically explicitly communicated. There is an opportunity here for coaching bodies to help practitioners in how they inform the client and customer about what is different at each level and address the difference in standard of reasonable care. Coaching literature is yet to embrace this point, and it is unknown whether coaches understand the implications of how they describe themselves and the meaning in practice of labels for different levels of coaching experience, such as 'master' coach (ICF, AC, EMCC).

Navigating this complex area requires attention. The coach sets the limits, and whilst this will be done in conjunction with the client and organisation, if relevant, it is for the coach to operate within their limits of skill and capability. This must be considered in relation to the skills and experience of the coach, at what level – or limit – they can ethically operate, and what standard is expected. For the coach to set the limits, they must be aware of their own professional limits and what to do in the situation where a client's needs go beyond their level of competency, for example, on matters relating to a client's mental health (Evans-Krimme and Passmore, 2023).

There is a growing awareness of the critical role mental health plays and the overlap between coaching and therapy. For example, coaches need to recognise when a client's needs extend beyond the limits of the coach's capability and the client requires professional therapeutic support instead. This may involve the coach stopping the coaching if their capability does not meet the client's needs, or postponing until the client has received the needed help and support and is ready to come back to coaching (Evans-Krimme and Passmore, 2023). The coach needs to be aware and to act.

Extreme situations where there are concerns of self-harm or suicide require fast action by the coach, who needs to signpost the client to mental health support as part of the initial coaching agreement (Evans-Krimme and Passmore, 2023). Evans-Krimme and Passmore (2023) make the important point that the welfare of others in the coaching relationship must supersede the self-interest of the coach. Let us not forget that.

This is an important reminder that it is not the role of the coach to diagnose. That said, we can equip ourselves with knowledge and understanding so our awareness is greater in recognising potential issues a client may be experiencing surrounding mental health (Evans-Krimme and Passmore, 2023). If the coach doesn't act promptly, indirect harm could be caused to others in the client's world (Evans-Krimme and Passmore, 2023). A further consideration is how the coach must aim for equality for all. Although mental health affects people across all demographics, gender, age, race, disability, sexuality, religious beliefs, cultural background, socioeconomic position, and others can increase the risk of developing specific mental health issues. These factors may also deepen an individual's experience of prejudice and inequality (Evans-Krimme and Passmore, 2023).

We know coaching has a ripple effect beyond the coach and client (O'Connor and Cavanagh, 2013). It is important that we pay attention, know ourselves, and understand our boundaries, our coaching philosophies, values, capabilities, and limitations. To help us with this, we can think about what we are bringing into the coaching dynamic and what type of environment we are creating.

In other domains such as nursing, the literature draws our attention to the type of environment and how practitioners create a moral climate, a climate with underlying and explicit values that guide healthcare delivery and influence the environments where care is provided. For nurses to deliver safe and effective care, it is essential that they operate within a moral climate, one that fosters ethical practices (Doane, Storch and Varcoe, 2006).

In sports coaching, the coach plays an integral role in influencing the moral terrain, striving to positively impact the situation, aiming to ensure that interactions within the coaching context are successful rather than problematic. The sports coach has a responsibility to establish a moral climate (Hardman, Jones and Jones, 2010; Lyle, 2019; Loughead, Patterson and Carron, 2008; Burton, Peachey and Wells, 2017).

However, as coaches, we are not providing care as nurses do, nor is it our role to positively influence in the same way as sports coaches do. Yet we can learn from these two fields in how we develop greater awareness of our own values, intentions, and behaviours and how we can gain greater clarity on what our ethical obligations are as practitioners.

Considering ethically acceptable and unacceptable influence over others allows the coach to assess the role they play in the coaching relationship and to what degree they influence their client and their client's action. It is for the coach to actively interrogate and reflect on their own practice and their understanding of themselves, their capability, and the scope of their role. This does not mean organisational stakeholders absolve themselves of responsibility. But as we know from ancient philosophy through to current thinking, we can only control our own reactions, behaviours, and actions and not those of others. So, it is up to us to be aware of ourselves and consider how we can create an environment for coaching that is conducive to meeting the client's needs.

Knowing oneself as a practitioner

I started this chapter by using the metaphor of a dance, a question of who takes the lead in the delicate and transformative dance of coaching. The steps will not be the same – each interaction is different and unique. The coach must adapt in the moment, drawing upon a deep understanding of themselves and their values to guide the process. This self-awareness helps the coach to be fully present and responsive, allowing them to navigate the dynamic flow of the coaching relationship with congruence between themselves and the client. By knowing themselves, recognising biases, emotions, and intentions, coaches are better equipped to create an environment where the client feels supported, understood, and safe, ultimately fostering growth and development.

This book does not offer process nor tick lists for a practitioner to follow, and this is a deliberate decision, as coaching is not mechanical – there is no single process that covers all. Given the significant levels of complexity and uncertainty in our relational work as coaches, we cannot depend solely on models of practice, however compelling they may seem (Jackson and Bachkirova, 2018). Our work is inherently value laden and is deeply personal for our clients (Iordanou et al., 2017), making it impossible for us to adopt a purely mechanical approach (Jackson and Bachkirova, 2018).

If we adopt the principle that the coach is the main instrument in the coaching process (Bachkirova, 2016), the coach has a duty to understand their role and the work they are in and to critically evaluate it. They must also understand themselves, develop their own reflexivity, understand their values and principles, and develop a practice that aligns with them as a person (Jackson and Bachkirova, 2018). Each coach is different, and the uniqueness of coaching requires the coach to meet the unique needs of each client (Bachkirova, 2016). To do this requires an appreciation of who we are as people. Our own lived experiences are different from those of others. Our norms are different. For example, I am a white woman, living in the northern hemisphere, with western norms. My lived experience is completely different from that of someone from a different background or race. We have to understand this and raise our awareness; otherwise, we can unintentionally cause harm.

As a coach and coach supervisor, I reflect regularly on my own practice, being mindful of what has changed in my own life and how that affects how I show up in the world. This reflection comes from three phenomenological perspectives – my philosophy of coaching and supervision, my purpose as a coach and supervisor, and what I do in practice that supports these first two (Jackson and Bachkirova, 2018). The exercise in Chapter 1 can inform some of these elements, and I encourage the reader to pause and reflect on their own practice in relation to the discussion in this chapter on boundaries and standards.

Concluding thoughts

If we are to operate ethically as practitioners, we must do so with an appreciation of what's needed on a practical level, with agreements in place. Second, the less tangible but important elements of managing and maintaining boundaries and standards, including matters relating to mental health, are integral. Finally, for us to be better equipped at succeeding in our roles, we must develop an understanding and awareness of ourselves and keep coming back to this and reflecting on it.

It starts with us.

References

Bachkirova, T. (2016) 'The self of the coach: Conceptualization, issues, and opportunities for practitioner development', *Consulting Psychology Journal: Practice and Research*, 68(2), pp. 143–156. https://doi.org/10.1037/cpb0000055

Bachkirova, T. and Baker, S. (2018) 'Revisiting the issue of boundaries between coaching and counselling', In *Handbook of coaching psychology: A guide for practitioners*. 2nd Ed. London: Routledge, Taylor and Francis Group. pp. 487–499.

Bond, T. (2015) *Standards and ethics for counselling in action*. 4th Ed. London: Sage. p. 306. *Book*. 2nd Ed. Thousand Oaks, CA: Sage.

Brennan, D. and Wildflower, L. (2018) 'Ethics in coaching', In *The complete handbook of coaching*, eds. E. Cox, T. Bachkirova, and D. Clutterbuck. 3rd Ed. London: Sage. pp. 500–517.

Burton, L., Peachey, J. and Wells, J. (2017) 'The role of servant leadership in developing an ethical climate in sport organizations', *Journal of Sport Management*, 31(3), pp. 229–240. https://doi.org/10.1123/jsm.2016-0047

Cassidy, T., Jones, R. and Potrac, P. (2015) *Understanding sports coaching: The pedagogical, social and cultural foundations of coaching practice*. London: Routledge, Taylor and Francis Group. https://doi.org/10.4324/9780203797952

Doane, G.H., Storch, J. and Varcoe, C. (2006) 'Toward a safer moral climate', *The Canadian Nurse*, 102(8), p. 24.

Evans-Krimme, R. and Passmore, J. (2023) 'Ethics in mental health and suicide management in coaching', In *The ethical coaches' handbook*. London: Routledge, Taylor and Francis Group. pp. 193–214. https://doi.org/10.4324/9781003277729-13

Farr, J. and Shepheard, M. (2018) 'Systemic constellations approach to coaching and coaching psychology practice', In *Handbook of coaching psychology: A guide for practitioners*. 2nd Ed. London: Routledge, Taylor and Francis Group. pp. 311–323. https://doi.org/10.4324/9781315820217

Gettman, H., Edinger, S. and Wouters, K. (2019) 'Assessing contracting and the coaching relationship: Necessary infrastructure?' *International Journal of Evidence Based Coaching & Mentoring*, 17(1). https://doi.org/10.24384/0nfx-0779

Gutheil, T. and Simon, R. (2002) 'Non-sexual boundary crossings and boundary violations: The ethical dimension', *Psychiatric Clinics*, 25(3), pp. A585–A592. https://doi.org/10.1016/s0193-953x(01)00012-0

Hardman, A., Jones, C., and Jones, R. (2010) 'Sports coaching, virtue ethics and emulation', *Physical Education and Sport Pedagogy*, 15(4), pp. 345–359. https://doi.org/10.1080/17408980903535784

Iordanou, I., Hawley, R. and Iordanou, C. (2017) *Values and ethics in coaching*. London: Sage. https://doi.org/10.4135/9781473983755

Jackson, P. and Bachkirova, T. (2018) 'The 3Ps of supervision and coaching: Philosophy, purpose and process', In *The heart of coaching supervision. Working with reflection and self-care*. Abingdon: Routledge. pp. 20–40.

Kitchin, L. (2024) 'The boundary and overlap with therapy in executive coaching-A study using Q methodology', *International Journal of Evidence Based Coaching & Mentoring*, 22. https://doi.org/10.24384/fned-mr57

Lancer, N., Clutterbuck, D. and Megginson, D. (2016) *Techniques for coaching and mentoring*. 2nd Ed. New York: Routledge. https://doi.org/10.4324/9781315691251

Lawrence, P. (2021) *Coaching systemically: Five ways of thinking about systems*. London: Routledge/Taylor & Francis Group (Essential coaching skills and knowledge). https://doi.org/10.4324/9780429356001

Lee, R. (2013) 'The role of contracting in coaching: Balancing individual client and organizational issues', In *The Wiley-Blackwell handbook of the psychology of coaching and mentoring*, eds. J. Passmore, D.B. Peterson, and T. Freire. Wiley Blackwell. pp. 40–57. https://doi.org/10.1002/9781118326459.ch3

Lefstein, A., Vedder-Weiss, D., Tabak, I. and Segal, A. (2018) 'Learner agency in scaffolding: The case of coaching teacher leadership', *International Journal of Educational Research*, 90, pp. 209–222. https://doi.org/10.1016/j.ijer.2017.11.002

Loughead, T., Patterson, M. and Carron, A. (2008) 'The impact of fitness leader behaviours and cohesion on an exerciser's affective state', *International Journal of Sport and Exercise Psychology*, 6(1), pp. 53–68. https://doi.org/10.1080/1612197X.2008.9671854

Louis, D. and Fatien Diochon, P. (2014) 'Educating coaches to power dynamics: Managing multiple agendas within the triangular relationship', *Journal of Psychological Issues in Organizational Culture*, 5(2), pp. 31–47. https://doi.org/10.1002/jpoc.21140

Louis, D. and Fatien Diochon, P. (2019) *Complex situations in coaching: A critical case-based approach*. Routledge. https://doi.org/10.4324/9780429056185

Lyle, J. (2019) 'What is ethical coaching?', *International Journal of Coaching Science*, 13(1).

Mayhead, B. (2022) 'Duty of care in coaching: From ethical frameworks to the development of the coach', Doctoral thesis. Oxford Brookes University. https://doi.org/10.24384/sjmq-9b67

O'Connor, S. and Cavanagh, M. (2013) 'The coaching ripple effect: The effects of developmental coaching on wellbeing across organisational networks', *Psychology of Well-Being: Theory, Research and Practice*, 3(1), pp. 1–23. https://doi.org/10.1186/2211-1522-3-2

Popovic, N. and Boniwell, I. (2007) 'Personal consultancy: An integrative approach to one-to-One talking practices,' *International Journal of Evidence Based Coaching and Mentoring*, 1, pp. 24–29. https://doaj.org/article/60379dcb486b44c09208d76af8dd66ff

Roberts, V. and Brunning, H. (2018) 'Psychodynamic and systems-psychodynamics coaching', In *Handbook of coaching psychology: A guide for practitioners*. 2nd Ed. London: Routledge, Taylor and Francis Group.

Sturdy, A., Clark, T., Fincham, R. and Handley, K. (2009) 'Between innovation and legitimation – boundaries and knowledge flow in management consultancy', *Organization*, 16(5), pp. 627–653. https://doi.org/10.1177/135050840933

Western, S. (2012) *Coaching and mentoring: A critical text*. Sage. https://doi.org/10.4135/9781446251577

Wilson, S. (2019) 'Transactional analysis approaches to coaching', In *Handbook of coaching psychology: A guide for practitioners*. 2nd Ed. London: Routledge, Taylor and Francis Group. pp. 297–310.

4 Contracting as a coach

Introduction

The first chapters of the book have drawn our attention to the background of duty of care and how our knowledge from related helping professions has helped shape our own codes of ethics and requirements. I shared how coaches draw on lived experiences, their sense of right and wrong, and their values when formulating their own sensemaking of duty of care. We know also that the law underpins our work and that written agreements are a necessary element in the work we conduct, including when we are working for no fee.

In this chapter, our attention is drawn to the art of contracting, the part of coaching often conversational in nature which paves the way in which the parties in the coaching relationship will be working. In Chapter 3 we looked at boundaries and standards, both of which are elements the coach will 'contract' for alongside the coach's written agreements of services. As we are working at a human level, we have a greater degree of responsibility, beyond the formal contractual, administrative side of an engagement. Contracting can often be a separate part of the process, providing an opportunity for all parties to agree roles, responsibilities, and boundaries. The coach has a duty of care to the various parties in the coaching relationship, and contracting provides the coach with an opportunity to ensure this is explored and that there is clarity.

Contracting happens at the start of the coaching engagement, before the work begins, and it happens throughout the relationship. It also happens at the start of each coaching session, a point where both coach and client set the boundaries for the session ahead, instead of diving into the work immediately. It provides those in the coaching relationship with the opportunity of ensuring there is clarity and understanding on what the client and customer want to focus on. Without engaging in contracting, there is a risk that needs are not met and assumptions can be incorrectly made.

DOI: 10.4324/9781003502494-5

From my own experience as a coach supervisor, and also as a coach, I've seen many ethical dilemmas that could have been avoided had contracting been more thorough. By having robust contracting, we can help ourselves and all those in the coaching relationship. Let's consider first of all who the parties are in the coaching relationship. We have the coach, the person who will be conducting the work. We then have the client, the person who is being coached. For coaches working in an organisational context, the organisation (the customer) may have commissioned the work (regardless of whether fees are being paid). There may be other people in the customer's organisation, for example, the line leader or human resources. These also become part of the coaching relationship. Coaches who work as associates for other coaching firms will also have them in the coaching relationship. Suddenly, the coaching relationship can be quite complex and crowded.

As coaches, it is up to us to first of all establish clearly for ourselves who is in the coaching relationship and what type of involvement they will have. It is helpful for the coach to seek understanding of perspectives, striving to align them as reasonably as they can, and to identify key differences, also acknowledging the requirement of constantly maintaining this balance (Lee, 2013). Contracting is a vital step, and continuing to contract throughout helps mitigate risks and avoid ethical dilemmas.

What is contracting?

Let's start by establishing a clearer understanding of what we mean by the term 'contracting' in coaching. In the context of a coaching relationship, contracting is acknowledged as an essential practice that can help avoid various ethical challenges (Iordanou, Hawley and Iordanou, 2017). Contracting is crucial, as it provides focus and purpose to the engagement, helping guide alignments between the coach and the parties involved, helping with understanding expectations and commitment, and reducing the likelihood of any misunderstandings. Importantly, contracting helps minimise ambiguity and addresses matters that might hinder the relationship (Lee, 2013). Contracting clarifies boundaries, the purpose of the coaching, transparency in communication, and outcomes, if appropriate.

Contracting is not concerned only with the formal agreement of services and the time frame for the coaching, location, length and frequency of sessions, costs, and payment terms. It is also concerned with the subtleties of expectation on the part of the client, the organisation, and the coach, such as confidentiality (Iordanou et al., 2017). We must also consider the psychological contract, the unspoken and informal agreement which fills the gaps left by the formal contracting process and, since not explicitly stated, typically only becomes apparent when it is breached (Lee, 2013). The implicit psychological contract accompanies the explicit terms of an agreement, and ethical awareness of this dimension is important for coaches. Recognising and navigating the unspoken expectations can enhance ethical maturity, helping ensure clarity in the coaching relationships (McClean, 2023).

The process of contracting can be verbal or in writing and is often a combination of the two. It can be simple, asking what expectations the client has for the coaching, or complex and layered with multiple parts. Whilst we may have become attuned to contracting as a best practice activity amongst our own coaching communities, and the process of contracting has become more normalised in our roles, our clients may not necessarily see it in the same way. A noticeable disparity exists between coaches and their clients regarding views on the significance and value of contracting (Gettman, Edinger and Wouters, 2019). I recognise this in my own practice and recall times when the client has wanted to skip through the contracting stage of the process at pace, seeing it as a means to cover the basic factors. This leaves us with a question to ponder – how do we 'contract to contract' with our customers and clients?

Contracting starts before the coaching does. Before formal or explicit contracts can be established, the parties in the coaching relationship must agree to collaborate in negotiating them (Lee, 2013). A preliminary process is conducted, which may involve verifying the coach's credibility, for example, and evaluating the compatibility between the coach, client, and customer. This is the pre-contracting stage (Lee, 2013).

When entering into a new coaching assignment, many coaches adopt an approach whereby the client and relevant parties are invited to a contracting conversation – a separate part of the coaching process. This provides an opportunity for contracting to be very clearly marked, so all parties understand what is happening. It is a conversation that can happen outside of the coaching sessions, a conversation where the limits and boundaries are discussed and explored explicitly, and questions are answered. The parties understand this is a conversation to set the pathway and not a conversation where coaching will happen.

For others, contracting in a new coaching assignment may happen at the start of the first coaching session. The coach may use the first part of the coaching session to discuss limits and boundaries, confidentiality, and the purpose and focus of the coaching. This approach of discussing it in a coaching session for a new assignment will typically only include the coach and the client, unless a sponsor is invited for that part of it and then asked to leave once this part is complete. From personal experience, though, I have found that a separate conversation goes more smoothly.

Here's why I prefer it to be separate. When the client comes to the first coaching session, they are expecting to be coached; they are entering into the work phase of the coaching. The coach will need to transition during the conversation from contracting, where the coach may be doing more of the leading, to the coaching. Once the coaching has started, the coach will of course contract with the client at the start of each coaching session. But the initial conversation, when the bigger topics of limits, boundaries, focus areas, and confidentiality are discussed, takes longer and is more involved, which is why I prefer holding that conversation separately.

There is no mandate for how contracting should be done. It is up to us in our individual practices to establish how we do it and for us to ensure we have covered it adequately so the client and relevant parties in the coaching relationship are aware of the boundaries. Of importance are the focus areas, intentions, or goals for the client – an exploration of what the client (and customer, where involved) wants to gain from the coaching. Sometimes the client might need help in establishing what the focus areas are, and the contracting stage provides a space for this to be explored.

Roles and responsibilities of each party are covered, including what the client requires from the coach and what the coach requires from the client. In assignments where there is an organisation involved (the customer), it is important to define the customer's position in this process, how confidentiality will be managed, and in what circumstances confidentiality might be broken. This part of the process requires attention from the coach and an appreciation of the potential power dynamics, with an awareness of the risks of becoming a pawn in the organisational game (Vitzthum, 2023).

Coaches must understand their own levels of capability and expertise. During the contracting conversation, the coach may explain that in circumstances where the coaching moves beyond the scope of the coach's expertise, the coach may refer the client to alternative resources. Practicalities of location, duration, and cadence of coaching sessions are agreed upon, and how the coaching might be evaluated can also be included. Endings are also included, and Chapter 6 in this book will explore this intricate part of the process in more detail. As we can see, there are many areas which can be covered in the contracting stage, hence the merit of holding this as a separate conversation when entering into new coaching assignments.

Five key components of contracting are integral to minimising potential ambiguity and issues which might hinder the relationship between coach, client, and relevant parties. These are clear contracting, a transparent process, building trust, managing difficulties, and ensuring two-way communication (Lai and McDowall, 2014).

As the reader, take some time now to consider how you approach the contracting stage and whether adjustments are needed. At the end of this chapter, an exercise is offered to help with interrogating our own contracting approaches.

Re-contracting

We've discussed the need for a clear and robust contracting process at the start of any coaching assignment. However, as coaching engagements are live situations, dynamic in nature, with multiple moving parts, contracting is a process point that coaches re-visit and engage with through re-contracting. We are yet to explore this in research, and empirical data is lacking. However, we know from practice that coaches do build in re-contracting stages at regular intervals. For example, if a coach is conducting a six-month coaching assignment, they may build in a mid-way check-in with all parties, a formal re-contracting stage in the process.

Regardless of whether a formal stage is built in, re-contracting is an essential part of the coaching relationship. It's not a one-time event but rather a continuous process that helps ensure coach, client, and relevant parties remain aligned. The coaching evolves, the client may experience new and unexpected challenges, and priorities may shift and change. This fluidity requires constant recalibration, and we do this by re-contracting.

In my own research, it was evident that coaches considered re-contracting part of how they enacted their duty of care. They re-contracted regularly, even with multiple occurrences of re-contracting within one coaching session. By engaging in regular re-contracting conversations, coaches reaffirm their duty of care, creating space to explore new or changing needs (Mayhead, 2022). This process also serves as a safeguard, helping the coach stay attuned to emerging boundaries and challenges that may influence the coaching dynamic. In doing so, coaches are better equipped to uphold their responsibility while supporting the client in maintaining ownership of their own progress (Mayhead, 2022). Re-contracting isn't just a check-in; it's a vital component of effective and ethical practice.

As coaching is dynamic, re-contracting serves as a moment to redefine boundaries and responsibilities. Think back to your own experiences when during a coaching session the conversation veered into an unexpected or an uncontracted area. Perhaps the client brought up a sensitive issue or wanted to discuss topics which weren't part of the original scope for the work. In these moments, when the coach is conscious and aware of and senses the shift, they can invite a pause in the conversation. The pause offers a space to acknowledge the new direction the conversation is taking, and agreement can be reached on whether to continue along that path. This simple act of pausing and re-contracting demonstrates the coach's constant awareness of the boundaries and agreed-upon focus areas. The pause can be managed with gentleness and doesn't need to be abrupt. It doesn't necessarily disrupt the flow of sessions but can strengthen it instead. Both the coach and client can be secure in knowing there are boundaries in place that can be adapted as needed, with re-contracting ensuring that the coaching remains relevant.

In summary, contracting at the start of a coaching assignment is a vital step in the process, and it is common practice for coaches to also contract at the start of each coaching session and to re-contract throughout the coaching engagement. Additionally, coaches may implement milestone points in the coaching assignment where parties come together to re-contract more formally.

If you are thinking that your contracting needs tightening after reading this chapter, I suggest referring to the Global Code of Ethics, where very clear guidance is provided on what needs to be included in contracting. Let us now consider in greater depth some of those component factors which are important to cover.

Contracting for roles and responsibilities

During contracting, the coach can outline their approach, their role and responsibilities in the process, and the role and responsibilities of the client and customer, where relevant. As an example, dependent on the coach's own practice, this may include stipulating that they are not there to give advice but to guide and enable independence. The discussion might also include how much challenge the client wants, such as whether the client wants to be challenged by the coach, or perhaps they want the coaching to be more restorative. Again, all this needs to be agreed upon, with the parties in the relationship aligned. The coach can use this opportunity to share approaches they may use, and this may include discussion about any psychometric assessments or 360 feedback which may be included in the process. Clarity of understanding on the intent and the process for this and how the feedback will be conducted can be provided. It is much easier for all of these elements to be clearly communicated and understood at the beginning.

Without clear contracting and re-contracting, tensions can arise. In my own research, participants shared how most issues they'd experienced stemmed from 'loose wiring', as described by one participant, stemming from the contracting stage. One coach expressed regret at not having been firmer when tensions arose, and the nature of the relationship became complicated. Looking back, they felt they could have taken a stronger lead in clearly defining the boundaries between the roles of practising coaching and counselling, as the relationship became tricky when the client expected more of a therapy-type intervention, which was outside of the role and responsibility of the coach.

Tricky situations are common for all of us in our coaching work. What happens when the customer has commissioned coaching for a leader on a particular topic, yet the leader arrives wanting to work on something else with the coach? What happens when the leader arrives at coaching sessions which are paid for by their employer, and they announce to the coach they have decided to leave that organisation and want to use the coaching sessions to prepare for interviews? What happens when the coach can't contact their client and has concerns for their wellbeing? The coach's decision making when encountering these scenarios can be helped if clear contracting on roles and responsibilities, and those of the other parties in the coaching relationship, has happened in the beginning. The more we can bring the grey areas into the light, the more we can help guide the process and avoid ourselves becoming entangled in complex ethical dilemmas.

A key theme in contracting is how the limits and boundaries of the coaching are agreed on, a point where the professional boundaries of the coach's role are laid out (Iordanou et al., 2017). For the coach, this requires a clear understanding between themselves and their client on their engagement and the boundaries of that engagement. The coach needs to be consciously considering their actions and judging what is prudently expected. This is typically addressed in the contracting stages of coaching (Lee, 2013; Cox, Bachkirova and Clutterbuck, 2018; Gettman et al., 2019).

Contracting for confidentiality

As coaches, our relationships are built on trust with our clients and our customers. Being very clear on how confidentiality is managed is one of the ways we can ensure that trust is maintained. This is another vital part of the contracting stage where we can outline to the client and customer how we maintain the strictest levels of confidentiality with all client and customer information, with the exception of releasing information required by law. The Global Code of Ethics provides guidance in this regard. It is essential that we establish clear agreements with clients and customers regarding the circumstances in which confidentiality cannot be maintained, such as illegal activities or situations where there is a risk to the client or others.

Contracting for confidentiality includes the coach's management, storage, and disposal of client-related data, both paper and digital records, while complying with the applicable relevant laws. For coaches who are engaging in supervision, contracting for confidentiality includes informing clients that they may be discussed anonymously within that context and that the supervisory relationship itself remains confidential. If coaches are working with vulnerable adults or children, they must work with the client's sponsors or guardians to ensure confidentiality is maintained appropriately in line with relevant laws and safeguarding practices and in the client's best interests.

A common scenario experienced by coaches occurs when the client's organisation asks the coach to break confidentiality to provide information or feedback. This situation can be avoided by ensuring clear boundaries are contracted early on in coaching relationships about what would be shared and what would not. Even so, requests still happen, unlike in clinical professions, for example, where it is more commonly accepted that nothing would be shared (Mayhead, 2022).

Contracting for access to the coach

We must also consider how we contract for access to the coach. A coach has a responsibility to manage the access the client and customer have to them and their availability to the client and customer. Boundaries of access to the coach and modes of how these boundaries are set differ from coach to coach, unique to each coaching relationship. As previously discussed, contracting is concerned with setting the boundaries in relation to the limits of the coaching engagement, and this includes access. For some coaches, being available 24 hours every day through text messaging and WhatsApp forms part of their enactment of their duty of care, whereas other coaches might only correspond through email and during working hours.

The coach can also manage expectations with clear guidelines on response times for messages, emails, or other forms of communication. This can include stipulating time frames for response during working hours and not being available during weekends or holiday periods, unless otherwise agreed upon. The coach can include clear guidelines on the primary communication channel, for example, email for non-urgent matters, but can invite the client to phone or message for anything that is urgent. Let us not forget time zone differences and differences in public holidays and days of rest. For example, rest days are different for coaches from Europe or the US working with clients in the Middle East, so will the coach be available on Sundays, a normal working day for their client? Again, being clear and upfront saves misunderstanding further down the line.

Contracting for where and how

Since the world experienced the impact of the COVID global pandemic, much has changed in how we conduct business. A new norm suddenly became part of our world – virtual working. This has opened up access to coach and client relationships, as we are no longer restricted to location. Contracting with clients on how and where coaching will be conducted is another factor which can help ensure clarity of expectations.

Agreement at the start of an engagement will often include the number of sessions, their duration, and also the mode. If the coaching is happening online, the coach might choose to include some guidelines for the client to ensure they are taking the video or audio call in an environment which is free from distraction and where the client can speak openly and confidentially. The same applies to the coach. At the point of contracting for confidentiality, we should ensure we are in an area which is confidential, where conversations cannot be overheard, nor the client or customer compromised.

One coach interviewed during my own research shared how she upheld the importance of safety and had a strict policy of not conducting coaching sessions whilst the client was driving (Mayhead, 2022). Clients might say they are too busy and want to have a coaching session on the phone in the car when driving home. This coach considered that she had a duty of care not only to the client but also to the client's family. What if a moment of insight during the session distracted the client from the road and led to an accident? For that reason, the coach had a very clear policy that was communicated at the contracting stage (Mayhead, 2022).

When coaching is conducted in person, the same points on confidentiality apply. Ideally, coaching should be happening in private locations, an office meeting room or somewhere free from distraction and interruption, where the conversation cannot be overheard. However, this is not always possible, and coaches may be conducting coaching sessions in public places, such as coffee shops or outdoors. The coach has the responsibility to ensure they operate in the best interests of the client and customer and to protect the confidentiality of client and customer as much as possible.

Contracting for endings and letting go

Chapter 6 in this book explores endings in coaching relationships in depth. Before we arrive at that chapter, let's consider the role of contracting for letting go and ending coaching. Letting go of clients manifests itself in multiple ways, from a contract terminating to referring a client for support or stepping aside as the coach (Mayhead, 2022). It is possible that a particular coach may not be able to meet a client's needs, in which case the coach has a duty of care to let the client leave if they think someone else would be able to do so. With few barriers to entry and no regulation in the applied discipline of coaching, it is again up to us as coaches to govern ourselves and operate ethically with a duty of care to let clients go if we are not the right match, rather than to take or keep hold of the business. Understanding our own limits and capabilities and developing confidence in ourselves to recognise when we can't meet someone's needs is a demonstration of our own duty of care and of operating ethically.

Coaches also have a duty to protect themselves. The impact of holding onto a client for too long can be detrimental and not in service of the work that has been agreed upon. We have to ask ourselves for what purpose we are holding on to a client and for whose benefit. Letting go of a client can be an emotional experience. The coach might have become deeply invested in the client's success, and there is a balance here in how the coach remains effective. In my own research, one coach shared how, even though they maintained professionalism as a coach, they experienced an inner moment of support for the client, hoping they would land the new role they were going for or experience a breakthrough (Mayhead, 2022).

A trusted colleague of mine, Dr Vitzthum, shared with me her perspective on the point of 'hope' as a coach. If the coach is working from a place of positive regard, it's *not* about hoping for the client's success, but it is about recognising that this hope shouldn't cloud the coach's ability to challenge the client or work with them through difficult decisions, even when those may differ from what the coach might personally hope to see. Dr Vitzthum's perspective provides an important lens for us all to consider.

Part of fulfilling our duty of care is recognising when the best way to support the client is by ending the coaching relationship. Sometimes, stepping back is the most caring thing we can do for their growth. One coach shared with me how their client came back to them and said, 'you put me first'. In that moment, the coach realised that ending the partnership was not a setback but an act of care that had a profound impact on the client (Mayhead, 2022). Sometimes letting go is the ultimate way to prioritise the client's wellbeing and long-term success.

Concluding thoughts

The process of contracting is dynamic and recurs throughout the coaching relationship. The coach remains attuned to the delicate balance of keeping the focus of the coaching on the client's needs whilst being aligned to agreements with other parties involved, such as the customer. Developing the capability and confidence to gently pause and re-contract is a skill which can help strengthen the coaching. As coaches, we have the opportunity to reflect and think about our own practice and consider what else we might add in, or take out, in how we contract and re-contract.

Your practice in focus

Take some time to reflect on and consider the following questions. Make notes on what you would like to change, what's working well, and how you know.

How do you contract with your clients?

What else do you think needs to be added to your existing approach?

Think back to a recent coaching session where there were opportunities to re-contract. What did you do in those instances?

Think back to coaching sessions where you didn't re-contract. What was stopping you from re-contracting? What do you need to do to remove that barrier in future coaching sessions?

Reflect back on a situation where you experienced an ethical dilemma in your coaching practice. How could contracting and re-contracting have helped avoid or reduce the impact of the ethical dilemma?

Are there some client situations you feel more able to contract and re-contract with and some where you feel less able? If there are, what do you notice about those differences in relationships with your client or key parties? What is the question you could take to supervision to help explore this further?

What do your clients and customers understand about contracting? What opportunities are there for you to talk to them about contracting and the need for it? How can you help them use similar approaches in their own working dynamics, for example, with colleagues or direct reports?

What changes are you going to make to your coaching practice to strengthen your contracting and re-contracting activities?

References

Cox, E., Bachkirova, T. and Clutterbuck, D. (2018) *The complete handbook of coaching*. London: Sage.

Gettman, H.J., Edinger, S.K. and Wouters, K. (2019) Assessing contracting and the coaching relationship: Necessary infrastructure?. *International Journal of Evidence Based Coaching & Mentoring*, 17(1). https://doi.org/10.24384/0nfx-0779

Iordanou, I., Hawley, R. and Iordanou, C. (2017) *Values and ethics in coaching*. London: Sage. https://doi.org/10.4135/9781473983755

Lai, Y. and McDowall, A. (2014) 'A systematic review (SR) of coaching psychology: Focusing on the attributes of effective coaching psychologists', *International Coaching Psychology Review*, 9(2), pp. 118–134. https://doi.org/10.53841/bpsicpr.2014.9.2.118

Lee, R. (2013) 'The role of contracting in coaching: Balancing individual client and organizational issues', In *The Wiley-Blackwell handbook of the psychology of coaching and mentoring*, eds. J. Passmore, D.B. Peterson, and T. Freire. Wiley Blackwell. pp. 40–57. https://doi.org/10.1002/9781118326459.ch3

Mayhead, B. (2022) 'Duty of care in coaching: From ethical frameworks to the development of the coach', Doctoral thesis. Oxford Brookes University. https://doi.org/10.24384/sjmq-9b67

McClean, P. (2023) 'The psychological contract in coaching', In *The ethical coaches' handbook*. London: Routledge, Taylor and Francis Group. pp. 117–130. https://doi.org/10.4324/9781003277729-8

Vitzthum, C. (2023) 'A pawn in the game? The significance of contracting in coaching with gender-sensitivity', *International Journal of Evidence Based Coaching and Mentoring*, (S17), pp. 3–17. https://doi.org/10.24384/jbdb-xv40

5 Care and coaching

Developing ethical maturity

Introduction

In this chapter we will explore how coaches describe a sense of having a duty *to* care for the work they do. Up to this point in the book we have delved into the meaning of duty of care, how we can develop our own understanding of it, and how the coach sets and maintains the standards and boundaries in coaching. We have also danced with the intricate art of contracting.

This next chapter brings our attention to a key finding from my research – how caring is a feature coaches align themselves with, yet is not to be confused with taking care of another person. Connected to this is how our ethical maturity develops, which we will explore in the second half of the chapter.

Care and coaching

As a coach, being in a working relationship with another human being brings a level of responsibility to take care in what we do. We have a duty to work responsibly and to uphold the law. Care in this context is not to be confused with being responsible for the other person, nor their actions. It is not for the coach to take care of another but to take care of their own actions and decisions in the work they do. One participant in my research explained that the coach must demonstrate care for their client and their own actions as coach and asked: 'if they didn't care, could they be coaches really?' Being a coach is a privileged position, a role with recognised responsibility. I tend to agree with this participant's challenge – how can we coach if we don't care? What are your thoughts on this?

Care features as part of feminist ethical theories, with ethics of care being relevant to business and organisational contexts (Machold, Ahmed and Farquhar, 2008). As adopted by helping professions, ethics of care emphasises the rightness or wrongness as an implication of interconnectedness,

DOI: 10.4324/9781003502494-6

emphasising the importance of relationships and their context (Iordanou, Hawley and Iordanou, 2017). In coaching, while we have taken insights from other related fields during our growth, the practice of coaching is often carried out within organisations, typically focusing on gaining a competitive edge. This emphasis can, in turn, lead to ethical dilemmas for the coach (Iordanou et al., 2017). It is important for the coach to understand the care needed to avoid such ethical issues.

Whilst competitive working environments exist, a shift has begun in the last decade with organisations focusing on happiness, wellbeing, and care for employees, with rhetoric centred on the type of organisational help required (Kirpik, 2020). This focus emphasises that stress is overwhelmingly present in people's lives and how it can contribute to loss of engagement and cognitive functioning during activities including training, education, and coaching (Boyatzis, Goleman, Dhar and Osiri, 2021). Indeed, episodes of renewal, such as caring for others and feeling cared for, are associated with overall improved health and wellbeing, with people feeling better if they have more episodes of renewal than stress (Boyatzis et al., 2021). Coaches can remodel development experiences to include more and an increased variety of renewal events to avoid learning being compromised by stress (Boyatzis, Smith and Blaize, 2006; Boyatzis et al., 2021). It is relevant that organisations' focus is changing, with more focus on care, which consequently prompts some thinking on what this means for us as coaches.

Coaching has become recognised as a way of helping people, yet excessive helping behaviour from the coach can be perceived as 'rescuer syndrome' (Kets de Vries, 2010). The risk of developing excessive helping behaviours could result in the coach becoming the rescuer (Diochon and Nizet, 2015). While 'rescuer syndrome' is not an officially recognised term, it is a phenomenon especially prevalent in the context of interpersonal relationships, coaching being one such relationship. Coaches have a natural tendency to help people (Diochon and Nizet, 2015), and they talk of their desire to do so (Mayhead, 2022).

Many coaches are drawn to the work of coaching and mentoring for genuinely altruistic reasons, and helping people comes with admirable virtues of compassion, service, and dedication (Korotov, Florent-Treacy, Bernhardt and Bernhardt, 2012). However, it is important how a coach recognises these potential inherent characteristics and how they explore their desire to help as part of their own development and growth (Diochon and Nizet, 2015).

Care in related professional contexts

As has been done in previous chapters, let's look at related professions and their understanding of the meaning of 'care', starting with nursing, a profession which is centred on caring (Scotto, 2003). 'Caring' has been conceptualised as a human trait, a moral imperative, an interpersonal interaction, and a therapeutic intervention (Beck, 1999). Caring is arguably more than just performing duties; it is an attitude of nurturing and helping another person (Scotto, 2003). It is also characterised as a personal offering, where someone brings their intellectual, emotional, spiritual, and physical human qualities to achieve a desired outcome (Scotto, 2003).

Whether caring is a virtue or an attribute and whether it is a conflated use of empathy and sympathy has often been asked (Noddings, 2002). The issue of control is often also questioned, suggesting that caring is not solely directed by the caregiver but is instead a form of shared control (Noddings, 2002). In terms of shared control, there are limitations with caring and complexity of situations, and the notion that someone can care for everyone is impossible to actualise (Noddings, 2013). There is a vast amount of research on 'care' in medical professions and areas of pedagogy, as well as in sports coaching.

Sports coaching has gone some way towards positioning 'care' in its literature (Cronin and Armour, 2017, 2019; Fisher, Larsen, Bejar and Shigeno, 2019; Dohsten, Barker-Ruchti and Lindgren, 2020). There is a need for the sports coach to establish an environment of care in sport, with reciprocity and mutuality being central (Agnew and Pill, 2021). It is also argued that coaching in sport should be redefined as an inherently caring activity. It is suggested that sports coaches should be provided with resources that demonstrate and explore how care is expressed in sports coaching, encouraging them to critically evaluate their own practices (Cronin and Armour, 2019).

Sports coaches' caring involves recognising an individual's needs and creating a caring environment focused on ethical principles of listening, taking time to interact, and engaging in moral issues to help meet individuals' needs, both as humans and as athletes (Dohsten et al., 2020). Indeed, we may recognise these behaviours in our own roles as coaches, mentors, and coach supervisors. The sports coach can demonstrate care through ethical means, and ethical caring is grounded in the belief that showing care is the 'correct way' to engage with others, carrying a sense of duty and responsibility to act accordingly (Fisher et al., 2019).

Similarities between us and sports coaches and how they engage with people appeared in my own research, with coaches recounting lived experiences of care being at the very core of their work and an integral part of their duty *to* care (Mayhead, 2022). Coaches experienced emotions with their work relating to their duty *to* care which often led to a feeling of tension, sometimes described as emotions of guilt, worry, or a burden they carried. Tensions can occur when a person experiences a pull between their different identities and when in challenging work environments (Caza,

Vough and Puranik, 2018). I recall the conversation with a coach who was a parent and who felt tension as their client was not spending time with their own children. Another coach who had been a senior leader could see the mistakes their clients were about to make. Both these coaches explained that because they cared, they felt for their clients, and this tension could at times be hard for them to manage (Mayhead, 2022).

In many circumstances, coaches use 'gut feeling', working on what feels intuitively right, good, and comfortable, often drawn from past experience and their 'emotional backcloth', which shapes the present (Fineman, 2003). My research found that coaches considered their duty of care to be aligned with a way of being as a coach (Rogers, 1995), with enactments of care going beyond what might be written in a code of ethics. Coaches described it as a process led by their character, which was shaped by their life experiences and values, rather than a conscious process.

Coaches describe how they enact their duty of care through demonstrating integrity and compassion, by sharing wisdom, being trustworthy, showing respect, and doing what is best (Mayhead, 2022). Virtues of having integrity relate to having a consistent commitment to do what is best, even when situations are complex and difficult. Compassion in the helping professions can be experienced as having disquiet and heartfelt care for another person's situation and their wellbeing (Beauchamp and Childress, 1994). One participant talked of pointing out potential hazards if necessary, using judgement on when to share their wisdom and demonstrating how they would critically think through moral or ethical issues and apply insight in the best interest of the client. Coaches found ways in which they enacted trustworthiness through being dependable, credible, and honest (Beauchamp and Childress, 1994; Kitchener and Anderson, 2000). They also demonstrated the virtue of respectfulness, mindful of having an attitude that showed consideration for others and an appreciation of how their enactments could have an impact upon another (Darwall, 2005). Yet they talked of worry for clients, a sense of tension in what to do at times, and an emotional burden they carried in some situations.

Emotional burdens in coaching

Emotional burdens experienced by coaches have not been well researched, with the nearest related sources in coaching literature being on emotional labour (Kemp, 2022). We can turn to other professions where much more is known, such as nursing and medical domains. However, nurses and medical professionals providing patient care are dealing with life-and-death situations, a world of practice which is far removed from our domain of coaching.

For those delivering patient care, emotional burdens can involve feelings of having provided inappropriate care, loss of control, and moral distress, with regret being a normal and frequently experienced emotion (Cheval, Mongin, Cullati, Uribe, Pihl-Thingvad, Chopard and Courvoisier, 2021). Worry can feature significantly, and the psychological impact of worry on medical workers resulting from the COVID-19 pandemic was evident (Pappa, Barnett, Berges and Sakkas, 2021; Blanco-Donoso, Moreno-Jiménez, Gallego-Alberto, Amutio, Moreno-Jiménez and Garrosa, 2022). Again, this does not apply to coaches in the same way, even though worry is a regular emotion coaches experience. However, it typically occurs in far less extreme situations than those experienced in medical and related professions.

Coaches express feelings of worry for their clients and consider carrying those feelings a hazard of the job (Mayhead, 2022). For example, there are times when a coaching session might result in the client being distressed. The coach might believe that their duty of care extends to fixing the client, that it is their responsibility to put things right. This is a tricky situation to be in. There is a point where the coach makes the decision about what to do without knowing what the future might bring for that situation.

Coaches shared how managing the worry required keeping a degree of detachment to avoid tipping into over-caring, as this could lead to the client being overly dependent on the coach. Too much care, and dependence on the coach could prevail for the client, with excessive attachment to the coach. The coach needs to have an appreciation of the risks of getting too involved. The burden could become heavy, even though the coach may believe the client is responsible for their own actions and for their own wellbeing – these are not the coach's responsibility.

Whilst coaches can safeguard against becoming embroiled in emotional dramas, they do still experience worry for their clients. Coaches described how they needed a certain detachment and how situations could become difficult if the coach was too involved in the client's issues. Being aware of the psychodynamics of transference and countertransference is important for coaches.

Transference occurs when emotions associated with one person are redirected onto another. In coaching, the client might be projecting feelings from past relationships onto their coach. These feelings could be either positive or negative and often stem from previous experiences or unresolved conflicts. This process creates a dynamic in which the coach comes to represent figures from the client's past, influencing the coaching relationship. Countertransference occurs when a coach redirects their own feelings toward a client. These reactions can range from compassion and sympathy to frustration or irritation, often influenced by the coach's own personal history and unresolved issues. Recognising countertransference is crucial for maintaining self-awareness and ensuring that emotional responses from the coach do not interfere with the coaching. By acknowledging and managing these reactions, coaches can gain deeper insight into the client's experience and provide more effective support.

Transference and countertransference are neither right nor wrong and are unavoidable. We need to be aware of them – our ability to recognise the signs grows as we grow. Working with an experienced supervisor can help us sharpen our awareness. We have a complex role and boundary point decisions for how to enact care in our work, checking on the client and ensuring the client has adequate resources to think about what action to take. Consider for a moment how you enact care in your role as a coach, mentor, or coaching supervisor.

Developing ethical maturity

In this next section, we'll turn our attention to how care as a coach plays an integral role in our own development of ethical maturity. First, ethical maturity does not equal the level of experience or hours in the field, nor does it equate to caseload size or complexity. Instead, ethical maturity involves the capacity to examine complex situations thoroughly while remaining unattached to specific outcomes (Bachkirova, 2023). It reflects an awareness that complete objectivity is unattainable, encouraging openness to different viewpoints and their critique. It also suggests moving beyond defensiveness, which can hinder understanding and personal development. Ethical maturity is a lifelong, ever-evolving process of learning, self-reflection, and adaptation, shaped by our lived experience. We don't just become an ethical coach; ethical maturity is something we must practice and reflect on, and we must do this repeatedly (Smith and Bretherton, 2023).

Ethical decision making in coaching is enhanced when the coach moves from single to multiple perspectives. The coach moves from total objectivity to considering the environment and motivation, from zero reflection to in-depth critical reflection, from simplicity to complexity, from subjective views to standing back, and from a blank sheet to awareness of the impact of prior experience (Carroll and Shaw, 2013). Ethical maturity is developed through an intuitive capacity which is rational and reflective when deciding between right and wrong. It is also developed through accepting accountability for ethical decisions made, which might sometimes require resilience or courage. It requires being able to integrate learning into our moral character and into future actions taken (Carroll and Shaw, 2013).

The flow of the development towards ethical maturity is continual. It is not a destination but a recurrent cycle adopted by the coach (Carroll and Shaw, 2013). The development in turn influences a coach's interventions, which are initiated from their own knowledge, their understanding of a client's situation, their psychological makeup, their own life experiences as a coach and as a person, their current worldview, and their own developmental stage (Bachkirova, 2016). Developing ethical maturity is one element in how a coach can further build understanding of themselves and how they align their personal values and beliefs through congruent expression of their coaching approach (Bachkirova, 2016). It is one part in the complexity of factors involved in coaching engagements.

Coaches can become entangled in the complexity of the web of multiple stakeholders (Pichault, Diochon and Nizet, 2020). Indeed, the coach brings their own experience, individual qualities, ethics, and level of development, and so does the client. This is in conjunction with the context of the coaching – the organisational agenda, culture, and environmental factors – and the factors pertaining to the coaching relationship and process (Bachkirova, 2017). Developing ethical maturity is one part of the coach's developmental process and is relevant in the coach's sensemaking and enactment of their duty of care.

An individual's ethical beliefs and how they respond with what they ought or ought not to do in given situations are informed by past experience and learnings from parents, educators, and society (Kitchener and Anderson, 2000). Developing ethical maturity is complex and continual and requires a combination of five key factors (Carroll, 2018). The first of these five factors is the way a coach develops and demonstrates ethical sensitivity. This can include interpreting their duty of care through their personal values while recognising the importance of maintaining their own self-care. Ethical sensitivity can be reflected in a coach's compassion, empathy for their clients, and the intentionality of their thoughtful and caring interactions (Mayhead, 2022).

The second factor is how a coach makes discerning ethical decisions (Carroll, 2018). This can be supported by using others to help their arrival at decisions through reflective dialogue and in coaches' awareness of external pressures experienced in the complexity of the coaching relationships (Mayhead, 2022). Making discerning ethical decisions requires a slowing down of pace and taking time, so that the coach can access their feelings, thus creating a gap between deciding and implementing (Carroll, 2018).

The third factor is how the coach justifies and understands their decisions (Carroll, 2018), and working with a coaching supervisor can facilitate this. Supervision can offer the coach an opportunity for reflection, critical feedback, and growth. It could be beneficial for coaches to explore, during supervision, whether they are engaging in defensive justification or simply explaining their reasoning constructively. This reflection can help coaches differentiate between genuine self-assessment and defensive reactions, ultimately improving their ethical decision making and self-awareness in their practice and supporting their development of ethical maturity.

The fourth factor in developing ethical maturity is how a coach uses reflection and is honest, open, and curious (Carroll, 2018). Noteworthy was the experience of the coaches in the interviews for my own research as they reflected on the meaning of duty of care. For most of them, it was the first time they had done this proactively, and, as one coach shared, the experience had made him more reflective than reading a code of ethics ever would have (Mayhead, 2022). My intention here is not to refute codes of ethics at all but to share how reflection gives the coach an opportunity to expand perspectives beyond the written word. However, we are reminded that reflection has temporal modes, dependent on what it is the coach is reflecting on (Cox, 2013).

The fifth factor suggests that a coach learns to find peace with doubts and uncertainties, demonstrating self-compassion (Carroll, 2018). Coaching often involves navigating complexity and dealing with the unpredictable nature of human behaviour, and as we have discussed, coaches frequently carry a sense of emotional burden, grappling with feelings such as worry and responsibility. At times, it can be challenging for the coach to mentally and emotionally detach from their clients, holding lingering concerns about a clients' wellbeing or the outcomes of a session (Mayhead, 2022). By embracing uncertainty and offering themselves understanding and self-compassion, practitioners can maintain their emotional wellbeing, ultimately enhancing their ability to provide effective support for their clients.

These five factors provide us with the core of a cycle, a development process that continues as their ethical maturity grows. The coach moves through these component factors, not necessarily in order nor in a linear manner, oscillating between the elements. Wrapped around the core is a casing that the coach draws from, factors which are influential in the development of ethical maturity. The coach builds ethical sensitivity through awareness of themselves and of the harm and consequences behaviour can have (Carroll, 2018; Mayhead, 2022). Their duty of care is interwoven through their actions and behaviours, derived from their sensemaking, drawn from their values and life experiences, as we discussed in the early chapters (Mayhead, 2022).

Care and compassion feature as elements in how a coach develops ethical sensitivity – being sensitive to another's needs – yet developing awareness and ability not to tip into over-caring or becoming entangled. Ethical decision making involves the coach's ability to recognise external pressures and thoughtfully explore the complexities of the coaching relationship. This process is enhanced when coaches allow themselves the time and space to reflect on these factors, enabling more deliberate and balanced decision making. By taking a step back and embracing honesty, openness, and curiosity, the coach can reduce defensiveness and cultivate a deeper sense of awareness. And, finally, the coach can be at peace with uncertainty, able to let go, with compassion for themselves as coach. Central to all of this is how we use reflective dialogue, a space to explore and work through our thinking, most often with a supervisor. Reflective dialogue is a key ingredient in how we develop ethical maturity.

Concluding thoughts

We discussed at the start of this chapter how the subject of care is derived from feminist ethical theories, with ethics of care being relevant to business and organisational contexts. Ethics of care emphasises the rightness or wrongness as an implication of interconnectedness, with emphasis on the relationships and the contexts seen in the helping professions. It is a way of thinking about what is right and wrong based on how people are connected to each other. Instead of focusing only on strict rules, it emphasises relationships and the particular situations people may be in, an approach needed in professions such as nursing, for example. For coaching in organisational contexts, this raises questions, as coaching is often used to improve performance, which in turn can cause ethical issues for the coach. The coach might be required to help drive improvement of performance, often in competitive environments. The question of the coach's care comes to the fore, as the coach is not working in isolation but is entwined in the interconnectedness of the moving parts in the organisation.

For the coach, care is needed in order to avoid ethical issues, but whilst competitive working environments do exist, a shift has begun in the last decade, with the focus of organisations moving to employee happiness, wellbeing, and care and with rhetoric emphasising the type of organisational help required (Kirpik, 2020). Coaching as an intervention is used to help people and create episodes of renewal. Caring for others and feeling cared for are associated with overall improved health and wellbeing.

Coaches use reflective dialogue to make sense in their practice as coaches, and their development in relation to ethics is continual. Ethical maturity includes our ability to truly examine complex and often uncomfortable situations whilst remaining detached from the outcome. Complete objectivity isn't achievable, yet the more we can move beyond defensiveness, the more we can develop. We are in a continual cycle, with each coaching interaction being unique, and we have an abundance of opportunities to reflect and consider how our ethical maturity is developing.

An invitation is offered to you as the reader to reflect on the points in this chapter on care and the development of ethical maturity and to challenge your own practice. Perhaps you could use some of the points to take to peers, group supervision, or individual supervision for further reflection.

References

Agnew, D. and Pill, S. (2021) 'Creating caring environments: An exploration of football managers and coaching', *Sports Coaching Review*, pp. 1–20.

Bachkirova, T. (2016) 'The self of the coach: Conceptualization, issues, and opportunities for practitioner development', *Consulting Psychology Journal: Practice and Research*, 68(2), pp. 143–156. https://doi.org/10.1037/cpb0000055

Bachkirova, T. (2017) 'Developing a knowledge base of coaching: Questions to explore'. https://radar.brookes.ac.uk/radar/items/f15792ac-730f-45f2-b087-22b819be6239/1/
https://doi.org/10.1037/0003-066X.46.4.422

Bachkirova, T. (2023) 'Foreword: Where does ethical coaching start?', In *The ethical coaches' handbook*. London: Routledge, Taylor and Francis Group. pp. xxxvi–xliii. https://doi.org/10.4324/9781003277729-13

Beauchamp, T. and Childress, J. (1994) *Principles of biomedical ethics*. 4th Ed. New York: Oxford University Press. https://doi.org/10.1016/S0035-9203(02)90265-8

Beck, C.T. (1999) 'Quantitative measurement of caring', *Journal of Advanced Nursing*, 30(1), pp. 24–32. https://doi.org/10.1046/j.1365-2648.1999.01045.x

Blanco-Donoso, L., Moreno-Jiménez, J., Gallego-Alberto, L., Amutio, A., Moreno-Jiménez, B. and Garrosa, E., (2022) 'Satisfied as professionals, but also exhausted and worried!!: The role of job demands, resources and emotional experiences of Spanish nursing home workers during the COVID-19 pandemic', *Health & Social Care in the Community*, 30(1), pp. 148–160. https://doi.org/10.1111/hsc.13422

Boyatzis, R., Goleman, D., Dhar, U. and Osiri, J. (2021) 'Thrive and survive: Assessing personal sustainability', *Consulting Psychology Journal: Practice and Research*, 73(1), pp. 27–50. https://doi.org/10.1037/cpb0000193

Boyatzis, R., Smith, M. and Blaize, N. (2006) 'Developing sustainable leaders through coaching and compassion', *Academy of Management Learning and Education*, 5(1), pp. 8–24. https://doi.org/10.5465/AMLE.2006.20388381

Carroll, M. (2018) 'Coaching psychology supervision: Luxury or necessity?' In *Handbook of coaching psychology: A guide for practitioners*, eds. S. Palmer and A. Whybrow. Routledge. pp. 431–448.

Carroll, M. and Shaw, E. (2013) *Ethical maturity in the helping professions: Making difficult life and work decisions*. UK: Jessica Kingsley Publishers.

Caza, B., Vough, H. and Puranik, H. (2018) 'Identity work in organizations and occupations: Definitions, theories, and pathways forward', *Journal of Organizational Behavior*, 39(7), pp. 889–910. http://libres.uncg.edu/ir/uncg/f/B_Caza_Identity_2018.pdf https://doi.org/10.1002/job.2318

Cheval, S., Mongin, D., Cullati, S., Uribe, A., Pihl-Thingvad, J., Chopard, P. and Courvoisier, D.S. (2021) 'Associations of emotional burden and coping strategies with sick leave among healthcare professionals: A longitudinal observational study', *International Journal of Nursing Studies*, 115, p. 103869. https://doi.org/10.1016/j.ijnurstu.2021.103869

Cox, E. (2013) *Coaching understood: A pragmatic inquiry into the coaching process*. London: SAGE. https://doi.org/10.1260/1747-9541.8.1.265

Cronin, C. and Armour, K. (2017) '"Being" in the coaching world: New insights on youth performance coaching from an interpretative phenomenological approach', *Sport, Education and Society*, 22(8), pp. 919–931. https://doi.org/10.1080/13573322.2015.1108912

Cronin, C. and Armour, K. (eds) (2019) *Care in sport coaching: Pedagogical cases*. Abingdon, Oxon: Routledge (Routledge research in sports coaching). https://doi.org/10.4324/9781351109314

Darwall, S. (2005) 'Virtue ethics', *Australasian Journal of Philosophy*, 83(4), pp. 589–597. https://doi.org/10.1080/00048400500339003

Diochon, P.F. and Nizet, J. (2015) 'Ethical codes and executive coaches: One size does not fit all', *The Journal of Applied Behavioral Science*, 51(2), pp. 277–301. https://doi.org/10.1177/0021886315576190

Dohsten, J., Barker-Ruchti, N. and Lindgren, E. (2020) 'Caring as sustainable coaching in elite athletics: Benefits and challenges', *Sports Coaching Review*, 9(1), pp. 48–70. https://doi.org/10.1080/21640629.2018.1558896

Fineman, S. (2003) *Understanding emotion at work*. London: SAGE. https://doi.org/10.4135/9781446216538

Fisher L., Larsen, L., Bejar, M. and Shigeno, T. (2019) 'A Heuristic for the relationship between caring coaching and elite athlete performance', *International Journal of Sports Science and Coaching*, 14(2), pp. 126–137. https://doi.org/10.1177/1747954119827192

Iordanou, I., Hawley, R. and Iordanou, C. (2017) *Values and ethics in coaching*. London: Sage. https://doi.org/10.4135/9781473983755

Kemp, R. (2022) 'The emotional labour of the coach-in and out of the coaching "room"', *International Journal of Evidence Based Coaching and Mentoring*, (S16), pp. 185–195. https://doi.org/10.24384/H98Q-Q162

Kets de Vries, M. (2010) 'Leadership coaching and the rescuer syndrome: How to manage both sides of the couch', INSEAD Working Paper. https://papers.ssrn.com/sol3/papers.cfm?abstract_id=1722610#

Kirpik, G. (2020) 'The concept of employee's happiness in human resources management: A systematic literature review', *Business and Management Studies: An International Journal*, 8(3), pp. 2750–2775. https://doi.org/10.15295/bmij.v8i3.1517

Kitchener, K. and Anderson, S. (2000) 'Ethical issues in counseling psychology: Old themes – new problems', In *Handbook of counseling psychology*, eds. S. Brown and R. Lent. John Wiley & Sons, Inc. pp. 50–82.

Korotov, K., Florent-Treacy, E., Bernhardt, M. and Bernhardt, A. (2012) 'The rescuer syndrome', In *Tricky coaching*. London: Palgrave Macmillan. pp. 25–40.

Machold, S., Ahmed, P. and Farquhar, S. (2008) 'Corporate governance and ethics: A feminist perspective', *Journal of Business Ethics*, 81, pp. 665–678. https://doi.org/10.1007/s10551-007-9539-5

Mayhead, B. (2022) 'Duty of care in coaching: From ethical frameworks to the development of the coach', Doctoral thesis. Oxford Brookes University. https://doi.org/10.24384/sjmq-9b67

Noddings, N. (2002) *Starting at home: Caring and social policy*. Berkeley: University of California Press. https://ebookcentral-proquest-com.oxfordbrookes.idm.oclc.org/lib/brookes/reader.action?docID=223821&query=

Noddings, N. (2013) *Caring: A relational approach to ethics & moral education*. 2nd Ed., updated Ed. Berkeley, CA: University of California Press.

Pappa, S., Barnett, J., Berges, I. and Sakkas, N. (2021) 'Tired, worried and burned out, but still resilient: A cross-sectional study of mental health workers in the UK during the COVID-19 pandemic', *International Journal of Environmental Research and Public Health*, 18(9), p. 4457. https://doi.org/10.3390/ijerph18094457

Pichault, F., Diochon, P.F. and Nizet, J. (2020) 'Autonomy of independent professionals: A political process perspective', *European Management Journal*, 38(4), pp. 623–633. https://doi.org/10.1016/j.emj.2019.12.007

Rogers, C. (1995) *A way of being*. Houghton Mifflin Harcourt.

Scotto, C. (2003) 'A new view of caring', *Journal of Nursing Education*, 42(7), pp. 289–291. https://doi.org/10.3928/0148-4834-20030701-04

Smith, S. and Bretherton, R. (2023) 'Ethics, wisdom and adult development in coaching', In *The ethical coaches' handbook*. London: Routledge, Taylor and Francis Group. pp. 279–300. https://doi.org/10.4324/9781003277729-18

6 Endings in coaching

Introduction

So far in the book we have explored the meaning of duty of care in our roles as coaches and the complexity that lies within in it. As the reader, you have been invited to consider meaning and how duty of care is enacted, and we have considered the role we play as coaches in setting boundaries and standards. We have explored the art of contracting, and we have given attention to the need for us to develop care in our roles whilst being cognisant of the pitfalls in over-caring.

This chapter discusses the topic of endings in coaching relationships and our role as coaches in it. It tackles some of the issues associated with endings and debates why coaching sometimes does not end, or doesn't end cleanly but fizzles out instead, and the associated risks in this. Research on endings in coaching is scant, however, so once again we will look to other fields. The chapter ends with some reflective questions for practitioners for interrogating their own coaching approaches and their own personal relationships with endings. Drawn from my own research, coaches' lived experiences in relation to endings will be shared, with reflection on how we might consider managing endings as forming part of our responsibility as coaches, a facet of the enactment of our duty of care.

Endings in related professional contexts

In Chapter 4, we discussed the need for contracting and re-contracting in coaching relationships, whether the coaching is with an internal or an external coach. Part of the contracting stage can include agreement on when and how the coaching will end. For the external coach, a written agreement may form part of the process needed by the customer who is paying for the coaching, and this will most often include the duration of the coaching. For coaches who work individually and not in organisational contexts, endings

DOI: 10.4324/9781003502494-7

still apply. For the internal coach, how long the coaching will last might be agreed upon, or the coaching may be open ended.

Endings are a natural part of life at the various stages we find ourselves in. For the young child in western cultures, their time in education is marked by the start and end of years in school and progression on to the next stage. One stage stops, and another starts. Endings provide an opportunity for closure and enable a sense of completion before moving forwards to the next chapter. They mark the start of something new, including good events such as moving into a new home, starting a new job, a new relationship, or marriage. All of these events mark the end to a time before. Conversely, there are the more painful endings – bereavement, losing a job, a separation in a relationship, endings which sadly close a chapter in our lives (Bridges and Bridges, 2019).

Importantly, endings allow space for the next phase, for new beginnings and experiences. In the workplace, projects need endings to ensure time for evaluation of performance and deliverables. The ending of a project may involve handing over the finished product to a client, and well-executed endings can strengthen client relationships. Success can be celebrated and achievements acknowledged. Endings also allow a pause and reflection on learning opportunities, a transition point where feedback can be offered and ongoing development plans communicated. The phrase 'hindsight is a wonderful thing' is very true – had we known then what we know now, what might have changed? And what have we learnt along the way?

Related helping professions of psychotherapy and counselling draw attention to how ending therapy can at times be difficult for both the therapist and the patient. Both parties can experience a sense of loss, yet it is also a time to acknowledge the progress made. The parties experience mutual processes of attaching and detaching, of forming a closeness and then needing to say goodbye. These experiences can elicit powerful feelings for both therapist and patient (Salberg, 2009). We must also acknowledge a difference between therapeutic relationships such as in psychotherapy and counselling and everyday life – there is an expectation that the therapeutic relationship will definitely end (Fragkiadaki and Strauss, 2012).

When the ending is discussed several sessions ahead of the event in clinical or therapeutic settings, both parties can adjust and work towards it, avoiding an abrupt halt. It is suggested that 'termination can be understood as co-created enactments of complex unconscious processes' between patient and therapist (Salberg, 2009, p. 706). Therapists would do well to 'formulate what a co-created and mutually enacted good-enough ending would look like' (Salberg, 2009, p. 706).

Although the relationship ends, the bond between the therapist and the patient continues as they hold their relationship 'in mind' (Vanko and Roberts, 2020). The therapist holds the emotional connection and reflections from the work, even after the formal interaction has concluded. The therapist might carefully share their own feelings at the ending stage, yet keeping the patient's needs central whilst doing this.

In clinical and therapeutic relationships, endings can reignite and resurface painful feelings of loss and abandonment for the patient (Vanko and Roberts, 2020). The therapist and patient may have been working towards specific outcomes and the ending of the relationship from the outset. Ideally, the ending of the relationship occurs when these outcomes have been realised, yet this is not always the case. In cases where the therapy hasn't been successful, feelings of disappointment or regret can be experienced as what was hoped for has not been achieved.

Cox (2010) emphasises the importance of endings in relationships and discusses how endings in coaching differ from endings in related professions of psychotherapy and counselling. Cox (2010) informs us of the vital importance of the final phase in a psychoanalysis therapy engagement. The therapist interprets key insights and uses these as markers for deciding when the therapy should end. The therapist is influenced by their own theoretical orientations, anticipating specific changes or outcomes. Arguably, this gives the therapist a certain measure of power in deciding when the therapy will end. Whilst difference exists between the coach and client and the therapist and patient, practitioners on both sides may experience a sense of loss.

The relationship between coach and client does not have the same function as the relationship between therapist and patient. Both types of relationship can have depth, yet there is a greater emphasis on the depth of a relationship between patient and therapist and perhaps less so in coaching. This is in part due to the different types of coaching relationships. As an example, the internal coach may offer ad-hoc coaching sessions focused on skills development or perhaps live problem solving. However, the internal coach may also work over longer periods with a leader, and in this scenario, there may be greater depth in the relationship.

Similarly, in the escalation we have seen in easily accessible online coaching from global online coaching providers, the relationships formed between coach and client will not have the same depth as those of the executive coach who is working in person with a leader over a lengthy period of time. This is not a reflection on the quality of the coaching in any of these scenarios; the coaching may not necessarily be less or more effective. However, the depth of the relationship will differ depending on the nature of the coaching relationship.

The literature suggests that even if the relationship between therapist and patient does not seek to create dependency as a closeness is formed, there is potential for reliance on the relationship to develop (Cox, 2010). The therapist needs to forge depth in the relationship for working at a deeper level. This can cause both the patient and the therapist to experience a sense of loss at the end of the relationship. When a deep relationship has developed, the same can be experienced in coaching affiliations when the work ends.

Endings in coaching

The Global Code of Ethics states that members will ensure the duration of a coaching contract is appropriate for achieving the desired goals, and the coach is to work to promote the client's self-reliance and independence. The code states that the coach is to prepare the client for ending the coaching relationship, and the client has the right to end the engagement at any point. The coach is to encourage the client to terminate the engagement if it is believed the client would be better served in other ways. However, the code is vague and does not specify contracting for endings at the start of the coaching process.

The ICF Code of Ethics states coaches must respect the right of all parties to terminate the coaching relationship and to remain alert to any indications that the value received from the coaching has changed. The coach is directed to make a change or encourage the client to seek alternative resources. The ICF Code of Ethics also lacks guidelines for the coach in laying out the boundaries for endings at the start of the coaching relationship.

Endings in a coaching relationship are just as important as clearly defined beginnings (Cox, 2010). There is an inherent danger that coaching can drift, or go on indefinitely, which raises questions about whether coaching is meeting the business strategies or clients' objectives if this happens (Cox, 2010). Coaches differ in their enactments of ending coaching relationships, with some coaches being the decider about when the client is ready for the coaching to end. This approach has similarities to therapy, as the therapist envisions how the conclusion of therapy will unfold, influenced by the specific theoretical approach in which the therapist was trained (Cox, 2010).

If we accept that coaching is not the same as therapy and if the coach is the decider on when the client is ready for the coaching to end, this raises questions relating to the coach's duty of care and the level of power the coach has in the relationship. It further draws attention to how the coach views the client's agency, with potential ethical implications (Mayhead, 2022).

Whilst some coaches are clear on when coaching ends, some leave the door open for the client. This might be seen as being supportive of the client, but it could also be seen as encouraging dependency on the coach. Or it could be that the coach finds ending the coaching relationship difficult and thus avoids it. One coach in my research shared how she really didn't like ending coaching relationships and would say to the client 'the door is always open and to come back any time'. The door is left open, as the coach in this example finds it hard to close it. This raises questions about the coach's duty of care in relation to endings in coaching relationships – for whose benefit might the door be left open? In this example, it was the coach who found it difficult – so was this in the best interest of the client? We must also consider cultural norms and differences globally. For example, consider for a moment British politeness and how that might be driving the extension of courtesy to the client. It is perhaps prudent of us to challenge our thinking and ask what message we might be giving to our clients.

Who decides when a dyadic coaching relationship ends is a topic less debated in the literature. There are no established theoretical frameworks, and it may happen that the coach follows the client's needs until the client decides to end the coaching relationship. Yet this is not always the case, as my own research attests (Mayhead, 2022). In some cases, it was the coach who decided when the coaching would end. Perhaps pause now and reflect on what lies ahead for you and how you manage endings in coaching relationships. We will explore different approaches further on in this chapter.

An organisation's involvement in coaching engagements relates, amongst other parts, to what is contracted for – how many sessions will be offered and when the coaching will end. The process of coaching also involves addressing the conclusion of the coaching relationship. It is suggested that part of this process should involve a clear conversation about the timing and manner in which the coaching will come to an end (Iordanou, Hawley and Iordanou, 2017).

In team coaching, coaches ask themselves whether they should stop when the coach thinks they can add no further value or when the team thinks the coach has done enough (Hanley-Browne, 2021). The team coach makes this decision using their own judgement, drawing on key factors implemented at the contracting stage and expectations of outcomes specified to ensure a good ending to the coaching (Cox, 2010). The coach may experience a sense of achievement at the end of the coaching relationship but may also experience an emotional cost and a sense of loss (Mayhead, 2022).

Our own relationship with endings

Before we take a look at how endings might happen in coaching, taking a moment to explore our own lived experiences and relationship with endings can help us evaluate how we view endings in our coaching practices. We all develop or own typical responses to endings, either a mental state, a frame of mind, or a mood (Bridges and Bridges, 2019). When we think back to endings through our lives, emotions, thoughts, and feelings are conjured up, and we can notice our own style in how we dealt with them. We can ask ourselves about our own preferences for bringing things to a close. Again, we can see how our own experiences will shape our association with how we deal with endings. For example, the person who may have encountered abrupt or violent endings in their life may develop an aversion to endings by way of wanting to either protect themselves or others or avoid such situations.

In Chapter 2 we discussed our own sensemaking on what duty of care means to us as coaches, how we enact it, and how it is formed from individual lived experiences, our role models, and our values. The same applies to how we formulate our understanding of our duty of care with endings and how we enact endings in our coaching practices. Each of us will have our own experiences in how relationships and situations have been brought to a close throughout our lives. We recognise that we are likely to have found some endings difficult and painful. Some endings are brought about abruptly, and we may have a desire to deny the impact of change. Other endings are gradual, less noticeable. We can be active and initiating with bringing things to a close, or we can be passive and allow events to happen (Bridges and Bridges, 2019). Either way, endings are the clearing process for what comes next, both for the client and for the coach.

When I researched this topic, conversations with experienced coaches highlighted how differently coaches approached endings in their coaching practices (Mayhead, 2022). I have already stated that part of the coach's duty of care includes letting go of a client and ending the coaching relationship if that is the right thing to do for the parties involved. Letting go manifests itself in multiple ways, from terminating a contract, to referring a client for support, to stepping aside as the coach. A particular coach may not be able to meet a client's needs, and the coach has a duty of care to let the client go, perhaps to someone else.

Coaches have a responsibility to understand their ethical guidelines and to know when they can't work with somebody, when they can't meet the client's needs, or when there is a conflict of interest. This helps to protect both the client's and the coach's wellbeing. During my own research, one coach recalled how emotional they felt letting a particular client go and how it was the most caring thing they could do for the client. The coach recalled how the client acknowledged the impact of their own feeling that the coach was putting them first. The coach, in turn, experienced a deep sense of happiness for the client.

Coaches have different approaches to how they end coaching relationships, ranging from clear processes set out at contracting stage, with a fixed number of coaching sessions contracted for, to the 'leave the door open' approach. Let's consider different approaches and associated risks with how we end coaching relationships through selected short case descriptions drawn from research, and, as previously in the book, pseudonyms have been used to protect anonymity.

Case one

Joshua – fixed timeline of sessions

Joshua works as an associate for a coaching firm, as well as running his own coaching practice. Joshua has been coaching as an associate in a large organisation and has been following a fixed session approach agreed upon between the organisation and the coaching firm. Once a coach has been selected through 'chemistry meetings' (a meeting whereby a potential coach and client meet to establish whether they are a good match for each other, a mutual fit), coaching assignments start with a tripartite meeting between the client, the coach, and the customer. The sponsor is most often the client's line leader and sometimes HR. During that conversation, agreement is reached on how many sessions will take place. Midway through the agreed-upon number of sessions, a check-in call takes place again between the same three, and at the end of the coaching session, an end of coaching review call takes place.

Strict confidentiality remains in place throughout the coaching, with the coach and client working together and feedback only given by the client to their business – no feedback is provided by the coach. This ensures complete transparency for the coach and avoids compromising situations of conversations taking place between the coach and sponsor. During the end of the coaching review call, the coach facilitates the conversation between the client and sponsor. Questions are sent to both parties before the call, and the conversation covers what has been gained through the coaching, reflections from the client and sponsor on what has been noticed, and suggestions for what would help the client moving forward. Successes are celebrated, achievements are acknowledged, and the client and sponsor enter into a conversation on how the client will benefit from the coaching they have had going forward. Joshua shared how this approach removed awkwardness and provided a clear structure so all parties knew what was involved. He commented that on occasion he felt the pull on his emotions as the relationship came to an end, but having the end of programme review call allowed a greater degree of closure in a positive way.

Let's consider the benefits and drawbacks of this approach. On the positive side, all parties have sight of a clear structure and expectations for the coaching. Cost and time are managed clearly, and the organisation in this instance understands the financial commitment and time to be invested, which makes resource budgeting easier. The firm end date removes any ambiguity about the relationship's continuation and helps avoid the client becoming dependent on the coach. A fixed number of sessions helps encourage accountability from the client if they know there is a limited window for the coaching.

However, whilst there are benefits, a fixed number of sessions may cause a potential lack of flexibility. Focus areas brought to the coaching may require more time than initially anticipated, and a fixed number of sessions could restrict the coaching process, potentially leaving more complex topics unaddressed. Some clients may feel pressured to achieve goals or focus areas, which could reduce the quality of learning and reflection, resulting in only superficial rather than long-lasting change. Coaching is dynamic and a fluid process where new themes may emerge throughout. Having a fixed time limit may remove flexibility to adjust to these emergent themes. Finally, a firm end date could lead to a mindset of learning having been completed rather than growth being seen as a continuous process.

In the current economic climate, budgetary constraints are often the drivers of how long coaching is commissioned for. In our own practice, we have experienced sudden changes in contract length due to unforeseen budgetary constraints partway through an assignment, meaning sudden and unexpected change for the coach and client. This may include the end of coaching or the length of assignment being reduced. In such situations, it is the coach's responsibility to work to the best of their ability within the given framework and with the available resources to enable the client to end the coaching well.

A fixed number of sessions can offer structure, clarity, and focus, which could benefit clients with very clear and attainable goals. Yet this approach can also limit flexibility and may not enable deeper exploration for more complex topics. Ultimately, if entering into a fixed session approach, it is important for the coach to consider both the pros and the cons, the context, and the client's needs and to work with the client towards an ending.

Case two

Sally – the client decides

Let's consider a different case – Sally, an experienced coach. Sally describes herself as a fiercely independent person and someone who has had a hidden disability from a young age. She shares how throughout her life she has not wanted to be helped or to be considered helpless and becomes flustered when others try to take care of her. In coaching, she believes in the power of the person she is coaching, the agency of the other, and starts from the premise that the client is fully able to look after themselves. Her work tends to be at senior levels in organisations.

Sally mentions how she cares for the work she does and has empathy for the clients but does not confuse this with taking care of others – that is not her role. Contracting for her involves a conversation on when the client sees the coaching ending and what the client wants to achieve from the coaching, and this is very much led by the client, not her. The customer is also involved in this stage of the contracting, and agreement is reached on how long the coaching will last, again, led by the client and the organisation.

Whilst on a contractual level, Sally thinks she has a clear process for endings, on a personal level, she finds endings hard but at the same time strives not to avoid them. Meeting with a person every month for a year (a typical length of a coaching assignment for Sally) means relationships are formed; connections are made on a human level. She finds it's not possible to switch off the connection, and Sally recognises the same applies to the client. Her way of managing this is to offer extended support to the client in the last session, saying that if anything comes up in the future, the client can get in touch, and an ad-hoc session can be organised, in agreement with the client's organisation.

Sally's approach does leave the door open for the client, the client knowing they have a resource they can turn to, but Sally strives to set clear boundaries, including agreement required by the organisation. A courtesy is extended to the client and the organisation, offering future conversations if needed. This is a key point – it is about client or organisational needs.

This is very different to the coach who may use this opportunity to solicit business or extend the contract for commercial gains. Sally is very clear on how she ends the coaching relationship well, but not abruptly, and how the coaching starts with looking towards the end and the outcomes the client wants to achieve.

Case three

Alex – the coach decides

Another coach shared his account of his approach to endings, which involves his taking the lead on when the work should end. Alex worked in the corporate world for several decades before setting up his own coaching practice.

Alex shared an example of his coaching contract and how he regarded him-self as the decision maker on when the coaching would come to an end.

For Alex, coaching assignments can run for long periods of time – into several years on some occasions. Alex holds the view that if he considers the person he is coaching vulnerable, he will not end the coaching but will continue. Therefore, when coaching assignments start, contracting does not include a conversation on when the coaching will end.

In one particular case, Alex had been coaching a leader for a year. The leader had experienced tremendous personal challenges during this period, including the illness of a child and separation of a relationship. Led by his own values and beliefs, Alex recognised how his own experiences of losing his parents at a young age had shaped him and how this manifested in his coaching practice. Many are drawn to the work of coaching and mentoring for genuinely altruistic reasons, and helping people comes with admirable virtues of compassion, service, and dedication (Korotov, Florent-Treacy, Bernhardt and Bernhardt, 2012). However, how a coach recognises these potential inherent characteristics, how they explore their desire to help, and how this relates to their duty of care when ending coaching relationships are crucial to their own development and growth.

With this particular case, Alex did not feel the client was progressing, putting this down to the trauma they were experiencing outside of the work-ing environment. In his capacity as the coach, he talked to the client, explor-ing how they were finding the coaching and urging the client to continue the coaching. This is an interesting case fraught with ethical dilemmas, with the coach encouraging dependency on the coaching, as well as transference and countertransference of Alex's history with the client's current experiences.

Alex's own experiences of trauma related to endings had led to a position where he was holding onto clients and not letting them go. One perspec-tive to consider here is how the lack of endings brings the potential issue of excessive helping behaviour from the coach or of the coach exhibiting rescuer syndrome (Kets de Vries, 2010). Rescuer syndrome is not an offi-cially recognised disorder, but it is a phenomenon especially prevalent in the context of interpersonal relationships, arguably relatable to coaching. Help-ing others is a natural tendency of coaches. My own research revealed how coaches often talked of how they wanted to help, as was the case with Alex.

Alex's approach is fraught with issues and potential ethical dilemmas for consideration, centring on the balance of power in the coach–client relation-ship, the coach's responsibility for the client's development, and the need to respect the client's agency and autonomy. Stepping aside and letting the client go can be in the client's best interest. For the coach, taking these ten-sions to supervision and creating space to deeply reflect on the positive and negative impacts of decisions is a way of helping the coach navigate through the tensions.

Case four

Samantha – a co-creation

We've considered examples of how coaching can be for a number of fixed sessions, with a clear ending, or how the client or coach may decide. Coaching also sometimes fizzles out, with no parties discussing the ending – it just dwindles and stops. Or there are times when the client stops replying to the coach, and the coach makes the decision not to pursue the client. Who holds the power and the ethical considerations associated in such cases are points for us to ponder when thinking about our own approaches.

Samantha works with those in the coaching relationship to co-create endings, with open conversations at the start between client/customer and coach fostering a collaborative and transparent way of working. This approach is more aligned to the Global Code of Ethics and the ICF Code of Ethics. The client's sense of ownership and responsibility is enabled, with the coach mindful of supporting the client with access to what they need to move forward.

A co-creation of good-enough endings gives both parties the opportunity to reflect on the experience whilst respecting the autonomy of the client. The client remains responsible for their next steps and for applying the insights and tools gained during the coaching, should they decide to do so. This co-creation takes us full circle back to the contracting part, where both the coach and client are committed to upholding their respective roles and conversations take place on working towards a good-enough ending.

Concluding thoughts

As with many areas in coaching, we have drawn from related helping professions in our own understanding of endings. In clinical therapist–patient relationships, endings have a place in the process, and whilst different to the coaching relationship, we can draw some similarities. We know from the literature that endings allow for the new phase and are an important step in reaching closure, yet endings can also be difficult, both for the coach and for the client. There is a benefit in ending coaching relationships well, co-creating together with those parties in the coaching relationship, striving for a good-enough ending, and being clear on when and how it happens.

Your practice in focus

So, where do you find yourself as the reader when considering the examples shared on how coaches may handle endings? Do you take the lead in being the decider, or do you leave the decision with the client? Do you operate a fixed coaching session approach, or do you strive for co-creating the ending? Perhaps you find a variation applies, dependent on the coaching assignment. We can know from practice that there are different approaches. It is our responsibility to inter-rogate what we do and for what purpose and to question our decision making accordingly.

The following exercise can help us with exploring whether we are han-dling the process of endings ethically, effectively, and with the best interests of the client held as centrally important.

As coach, how have I helped the client achieve their goals or focus areas, and are there areas where they require further support? What might I be assuming in this? What might be alternative resources or support the client might benefit from?

What strategies or approaches have we developed together to help the client maintain progress after the coaching ends?

If the coaching is to continue, what are the reasons for extending it, are they the right ones, and are they aligned with the client's or organ-isation's needs rather than my own interests?

What are the potential power imbalances in how I am approaching ending the relationship, and how am I addressing them?

Have I allowed space for the client to reflect on their progress and celebrate their achievements?

What steps am I taking to ensure that the coaching relationship has a meaningful close?

What is my role in helping facilitate a smooth transition for the client to continue their development without me?

Have I considered the client's emotional state and readiness for the end of the coaching relationship?

Am I aware of any attachment the client may have to me or to the coaching process, and am I aware of any attachment issues I may have?

What support or resources can I offer the client to support their continued progress?

Have I referred the client to other resources or professionals if there are areas where they may need alternative support?

What can I learn from this coaching relationship about how I handle endings?

How do I feel about endings, and how are my own feelings and associations affecting my approach?

Do I have concerns about ending the coaching relationship, and are these based on the client's needs, or are they based on my own needs?

How do I balance my own emotional investment with a need to maintain my own ethical standards when it's time to end relationships?

What are the questions I will take to supervision in relation to endings?

References

Bridges, W. and Bridges, S. (2019) *Transitions: Making sense of life's changes.* UK: Hachette.

Cox, E. (2010) 'Last things first: Ending well in the coaching relationship', In *The coaching relationship: Putting people first*. London: Routledge Taylor & Francis Group. pp. 159–181.

Fragkiadaki, E. and Strauss, S.M. (2012) 'Termination of psychotherapy: The journey of 10 psychoanalytic and psychodynamic therapists', *Psychology and Psychotherapy: Theory, Research and Practice*, 85(3), pp. 335–350.

Hanley-Browne, R. (2021) 'What do team coaches experience at the end of a client relationship?', *International Journal of Evidence Based Coaching & Mentoring*, 15. https://doi.org/10.24384/PGFG-2005

Iordanou, I., Hawley, R. and Iordanou, C. (2017) *Values and ethics in coaching*. London: Sage. https://doi.org/10.4135/9781473983755

Kets de Vries, M. (2010) 'Leadership coaching and the rescuer syndrome: How to manage both sides of the couch', INSEAD Working Paper. https://papers.ssrn.com/sol3/papers.cfm?abstract_id=1722610#

Korotov, K., Florent-Treacy, E., Bernhardt, M. and Bernhardt, A. (2012) 'The rescuer syndrome', In *Tricky coaching*. London: Palgrave Macmillan. pp. 25–40. https://doi.org/10.1057/9780230362963_3

Mayhead, B. (2022) 'Duty of care in coaching: From ethical frameworks to the development of the coach', Doctoral thesis. Oxford Brookes University. https://doi.org/10.24384/sjmq-9b67

Salberg, J. (2009) 'Leaning into termination', *Psychoanalytic Dialogues*, 19(6), pp. 704–722.

Vanko, T. and Roberts, D. (2020) '20 Endings and the therapy relationship', In *Creative methods in schema therapy: Advances and innovation in clinical practice*. https://doi.org/10.4324/9781351171847-20

7 Adopting a systemic lens for duty of care in coaching

Introduction

Welcome to Chapter 7, which follows the exploration of the meaning of duty of care in our roles and how as coaches we set and maintain boundaries and standards. The intricate dance of contracting has been explored, and attention has been drawn to our care as coaches whilst being aware of the pitfalls of over-caring. We have also tackled the topic of endings in coaching and have delved into associated risks when endings are not happening.

The chapters so far have directed our attention to multiple parties in the coaching relationship. In the increasingly complex and interconnected dynamic we find ourselves in as coaches, we are entrusted with a privileged responsibility with our clients and customers. Our duty of care extends beyond the confines of the immediate client–coach relationship and is systemic, with greater reach to the customer (Mayhead, 2023).

As coaches, we have the opportunity to build broader awareness and sensitivity in the systems that influence our coaching practices and by the impact we have on those we are working with. By adopting a systemic lens to our work, we can increase our ability to develop a deeper understanding of the interconnected forces that shape us and the choices we make. We can begin to examine our own duty of care from multiple angles to determine how our work affects our clients in both their personal and professional lives, how our choices of tools and techniques fit within the larger contexts of our clients' systems, and how we ensure our own coaching practice fosters broader and sustainable change.

It was evident from my research that coaches had a sense of responsibility and regularly probed their own actions in relation to their duty of care. They recognised how their interactions as coaches with the client could affect change in a client's interactions, which in turn could affect others and society. They also had a sense of duty to the customer – some coaches suggesting a minimal amount, while one participant voice put the organisation

DOI: 10.4324/9781003502494-8

above the client (Mayhead, 2022). We know that coaching can have negative effects on clients and the wider system in which a client operates (Schermuly and Graßmann, 2019). Indeed, coaching has a ripple effect, creating an impact at relational and organisational levels, and not always in a positive way (O'Connor and Cavanagh, 2013).

We have an opportunity to think more broadly about this. Organisations (the customers) are invited to seek understanding of the complexities experienced by coaches. Collectively, we can aid the shaping of dialogue between the coach and the customer, thus ultimately supporting the client. Providers of coach training also have a responsibility in how they equip coaches to practice, and this part of the book is relevant to them, with an invitation to review their ethics training to explicitly include the systemic nature of duty of care.

In this chapter we will explore how adopting a systemic lens can support our understanding of our ethical obligations in our coaching practices by raising our awareness beyond merely the direct client–coach relationship. We'll consider how a systemic lens can sharpen our awareness of potential ripple effects and enable our decisions to be informed, ultimately supporting our duty of care to our clients and the wider systems we practice in.

'Systemic' in coaching

'Systemic', as a term, has become widely used in coaching in recent years, often without basis in meaning (Lawrence, 2021). Being systemic in its simplest form is to relate to or involve a whole system, with the system being elements which are inter-relational amongst themselves and with the environment (Lawrence, 2021). Let's break that down further. We are saying that being systemic means looking at how different parts of a system, such as a team, an organisation, a community, or family members, are connected and interact with each other and their surroundings. Instead of focusing on one part only, we consider the whole picture and how one part of the picture impacts and affects the other parts.

Being a systemic coach involves remaining aware of the wider context and environment rather than concentrating solely on the immediate issue at hand (Lawrence, 2021). The coach pays attention to what is happening more broadly – the coach is not actively involved in these occurrences, but they are there in the coach's peripheral vision. Indeed, to work systemically, coaches not only take a broader view but seek to understand what they are seeing (Lawrence, 2021) and reflect on what they are thinking. To be very clear, the coach is somewhat aware of what is happening in the system but is not coaching the system. Of course, the coach cannot be aware of absolutely everything, and this is not the aim. However, adopting a systemic lens for our thinking on duty of care widens our peripheral vision and allows us, in turn, to develop greater awareness of the impact of our choices and actions.

Systemic thinking is another term frequently used. It is described as seeing systems evolving and changing in relation to the wider system and beyond and how this is a continually moving interchange (Hawkins and Turner, 2019). This description creates the sense of an ever-changing dynamic between multiple parts. My own research was not concerned with exploring systemic coaching or systemic thinking (Hawkins and Turner, 2019; Whittington, 2020; Lawrence, 2021), yet participants described their awareness of having a duty of care to the wider system and not only to the client they were coaching. It is evident from my own work that coaches' perception of their duty of care was that it had a wider reach; it was systemic, encompassing all those in the coaching relationship and others in the client's system.

Coaching relationships often include the coach, the client (person being coached), and the customer (sponsoring organisation) (Athanasopoulou and Dopson, 2018). Indeed, these three are recognised as being in a typical triangular relationship (Louis and Fatien Diochon, 2014; Athanasopoulou and Dopson, 2018; Pandolfi, 2020). Whilst I do not contest that the triangular relationship is predominant in many coaching affiliations, coaches also talk of having a duty of care beyond these three entities. Coaching domains can have far greater complexity in relation to stakeholders in our contemporary world, with additional layers to the dynamic. These additional layers may include the typical tripartite relationship but also a coaching organisation if the coach is sub-contracted, the coaching field, the client's personal life, society, and the world more broadly. Ethical codes of practice focus on competencies and cannot equip a coach with how to deal with the degrees of complexity being experienced. Unless coaches move beyond reaching for a particular competency to solve an issue or following a list, they will remain in a linear mode. We have an opportunity to think differently (Lawrence, 2021).

Duty of care to whom in coaching?

If we adopt a systemic lens, we must first question to whom we have a duty of care. Whilst the literature focuses predominantly on the triangular relationship (Louis and Fatien Diochon, 2014; Athanasopoulou and Dopson, 2018; Pandolfi, 2020), not all coaches follow the principle of having a duty of care to all three entities in the triangular relationship, nor in equal measure. Some coaches believe their duty of care is only to the client and not to the customer, yet this is uncommon (Mayhead, 2022). Even more uncommon are coaches who consider the opposite, having a duty of care only to the customer and not to the client (Mayhead, 2022). This may surprise some of you as you read this, or it may not. We shall explore this a little further on in the chapter.

Coaches believe they have a duty of care to the customer and to the client as they are required to meet contractual obligations (Mayhead, 2022, 2023). For others, duty of care extends more broadly, with an awareness of the ripple effect of coaching. Coaching has an influence beyond the person being coached and an impact at both relational and organisational levels (O'Connor and Cavanagh, 2013). The impact can be positive or negative, with those on the receiving end of a coachee's changed patterns of interaction finding them at times less favourable than previous patterns, even though the coachee might rate themselves as having improved. Reasons might vary, including that there may be a lag in achieving competence, for example, in a particular new way of interacting (O'Connor and Cavanagh, 2013). I suggest we must accept there is a ripple effect from the work we do, either positive or negative, and that the impact is experienced by those outside of the direct coaching relationship. Yet as coaches we are most of the time unlikely to know the details of the impact.

> *I invite you now, at the start of this section, to interrogate your own thinking: to whom do you think you have a duty of care? Repeat the exercise at the end of the chapter and record what you notice about your thinking. Has it changed?*

In the next part of the chapter, we will begin by exploring having a duty of care through three systemic lenses: to the client and to the customer, to ourselves as coaches, and beyond these two. The following sections are illustrated by accounts and experiences of coaches shared during my own research. Pseudonyms have been used to protect their anonymity.

Duty of care to the client and customer

Above all, coaches recognise they *do* have a duty of care to the customer and to the client and appreciate that it is a contractual obligation (Kramer, 2003; Mayhead, 2022). You'll recall from the Introduction that the customer may be the invoice payer, the sponsor of the coaching, the organisation, HR, or the line manager. However, coaches also argue that their primary responsibility is to their client, the person 'sitting' in the room with them (Mayhead, 2022). Coaches experience a hierarchical order in terms of responsibility, with many considering they have a primary and a secondary responsibility. Most coaches consider they have a primary responsibility to their client – the person they are coaching – and a secondary responsibility to the customer – the organisation or the bill payer (Mayhead, 2022). However, we must remember the law is the law and must be upheld, regardless of what a coach may choose to consider.

Samantha, a coach who took part in the research, explained how she was there for the client, with her role being to support, encourage, challenge, and help in whatever way was appropriate. She shared how, in her practice, the organisation was secondary, and her primary interest remained always in the individual she was working with.

Like Samantha, who had the primary focus on the client, another coach saw his responsibility as ensuring that the client first took care of themselves as a leader before they could take care of their team. The coach saw his role as providing space for the leader to take off their mask and truly ask themselves how they were doing at that moment. The coach's duty of care was to the client but included thinking about the client's role in relation to the wider team. The client would bring accounts and stories to coaching sessions, and the coach gradually built a trusting relationship in which the client could discuss the issues that were affecting them, their team, and other stakeholders both in and out of the client's organisation. The coach recognised how these multiple parties were part of the client's entire system.

In this example, the system the client was in was ever moving and changing, and the coach had sight only of what the client chose to bring to coaching sessions. However, the coach was consciously thinking about these additional peripheral layers. The coach explained how it was his duty of care to support the client to better understand themselves and to think more deeply about issues they were challenged with and how to learn to become more effective.

When working with leaders in organisations, one coach shared how she enacted her duty of care by encouraging the client to get proper feedback from their organisation to ensure the coaching was not happening in isolation. Otherwise, she felt that, as the coach, she could unknowingly be supporting negative actions. She shared how the leader had responsibility for their direct reports, and she wasn't comfortable with what she, as coach, might be unknowingly supporting if she were coaching the leader 'in a bubble', as she described it, and the client was not getting proper feedback from those around them. She saw she had a duty of care beyond the client she was coaching and to the people around the client back in the business.

Contracting plays an important part in how the coach sets out to whom in the client's system they have a duty of care. This often includes a tripartite relationship between the organisation, the coach, and the client, as we have already discussed. But the actions a coach decides to take if they hear of something the client shares that could be detrimental to the organisation might vary. What is the coach's duty of care to the organisation – the customer – here? As a starting point, the coach might consider how they might work through this with the client to explore decisions on the course of action the client decides to take. But, whilst the coach may be bound by codes of ethics on confidentiality, there are circumstances where a coach may need to disclose information if withholding it could lead to harm. The coach would be facing an ethical dilemma. Codes of ethics do emphasise the importance of confidentiality but also state where disclosure is required by law. The coach must carefully consider the consequences of disclosure, and consulting with a legal professional or their coaching body would be advised.

In my research, most coaches saw their role as enabling improvement for the client, and if the coach did not consider they could make a difference to the client, they needed to end the relationship. Penny, another coach in the research, shared how if she felt she could no longer make a difference to the client, she would need to discuss it with the client and the customer. She held a firm view that as the customer was paying for the coaching, she had a duty to tell them. For Penny, the customer featured in her thinking about how she enacted her duty of care, how she had a responsibility to the customer, and how she needed to ensure the customer's best interests were fully reflected in the work she did for them as a coach. For her and other coaches alike, it was not acceptable to continue coaching and invoicing the customer if the coach and client believed the coaching was not adding value.

This point of adding value frequently emerged in my research. One coach shared how he grappled with reasoning on whether he had delivered value to the client or customer, for example, in coaching assignments where the goal of the organisation had not been achieved. In these circumstances, he asked himself whether the work he did was truly in the best interest of the parties involved. He'd ask himself if he could honestly say that the work he was doing with the client was to the client's and the customer's benefit. He shared how sometimes the outcome might not be the achievement of a goal-oriented target but could be a client feeling more competent and confident because of the process of coaching. In this scenario, he would feel at peace with having delivered to the client and the customer.

I want to share with you a different perspective, one which will no doubt divide opinion. See what you think as you read this next section. Although coaches, overall, put the client as the primary focus of responsibility, another view was from the coach who put the customer as the primary focus. One coach felt practitioners hid behind confidentiality and worked behind closed doors without sharing information with the customer, and this went against his philosophy of coaching. He did not subscribe to maintaining confidentiality and would openly share content from coaching sessions with the organisation. He focused on the measures of success and outcomes in complete alignment with the customer. However, a significant question here is what impact this approach had on the trust between the coach and the client when the coach openly shared feedback with the customer and did not hold confidentiality as core to the process. We must ask about the ripple effect on the client being coached, their trust in the process of coaching, and whether true work was being done. Or was the client too guarded in the knowledge that everything they shared with the coach would be fed back to the customer? Did the coaching becoming performative, with the client doing and saying what they thought was expected?

From my own experience as an executive coach, bringing the parties together to have open dialogue as a triad (coach, client, and customer) helps preserve confidentiality and ensures an openness and transparency in the process. These conversations are contracted for, and feedback and reflections are shared between the client and customer, with the coach present, at the interim point in the coaching process or whenever has been agreed upon. You may have a different view, and as coaches, we know from the early chapters in this book how our own sensemaking and enactment of duty of care come from our past experiences, our values, and our beliefs. I invite you to challenge your thinking on your systemic lens here: reflect on how you manage the dynamic between the multiple parties.

'Duty of care' to ourselves

We will turn attention now to ourselves, the coach, central to the system in the coaching relationship. The same applies to coach supervisors and mentors. Managing relationships with clients and our own energy as practitioners is something the coaches in my own research were cognisant of. They talked of how they had a 'duty of care' to themselves as coaches. It goes without saying, perhaps, that that is more of a lived experience, a phenomenological perspective, and not a duty of care in its legal form.

The nature of coaching dictates that coaches connect with people on a personal level and that the relationships they build have the trust of the client (Bachkirova, 2016). The client's trust stems not only from the coach's expertise and abilities but also from a sense that the coach is a genuinely supportive and trustworthy person (Bachkirova, 2016). Achieving this requires the coach to understand themselves and have congruence between who they are and the coaching approach they take. It requires the coach to look after themselves, thus sustaining their energy, and also to check for self-deception and bad habits in their practice (Bachkirova, 2016). Coaches in my own research concurred, as a majority recognised the importance of self-care and the duty they had in how they would 'show up' in coaching.

The internal coach has a different set of challenges with duty of care to themselves. The internal coach may be coaching in person or virtually, the same as an external coach. However, an external coach may visit clients to coach in person, perhaps spending a period of time on site before moving on. Yet the external coach has less attachment to the client's organisation and is most often less known by other people in that business. They glide in and out, often unnoticed. When a coaching session finishes, they might leave the client's office and perhaps head to their next appointment. Or if they are coaching multiple people in one client location, they can take time in between sessions to re-set and re-charge energy – alone.

For the internal coach who is coaching in person, their experience can be very different. An internal coach shared with me how he rarely found time to re-set and re-energise when coaching in person. After finishing a session, he would leave the meeting room and enter the general working area where he was very well known. Immediately he would find himself in conversations and engaging with other people. He recognised this and therefore ensured that he did not have multiple coaching sessions back-to-back. He described being ready to coach as having his ears sharp. If he had been pulled in between sessions into business related topics, he would not get this opportunity. His duty of care to himself was enacted through spacing out sessions, ensuring longer gaps in between when coaching in person, and he had found that coaching online afforded him greater control in managing his energy and attention.

Widely acknowledged across the coaches in my own research was how their duty of care extended also to themselves as coaches. Coaches spoke of putting on their own oxygen mask first – the analogy used in aircraft safety briefings where passengers are told to tend to their own need for oxygen before helping others. As coaches themselves, they recognised the need to ensure that they were in a good state, that they were not feeling threatened or stressed.

Coaching is complex, with boundaries not always clearly defined. As coaches, deciding what is in and out of an area of expertise is more accessible when we are free from stress or threat ourselves. Otherwise, maintaining boundaries and remaining safe are more difficult to achieve. Reflective practice and supervision help with this, and we'll discuss this in much greater detail in Chapter 8. But briefly for now, supervision can help the coach focus on how they help themselves, how they put their own oxygen mask on first. We may find times when we pay less attention to ourselves than we do to our clients.

We are complex human beings in the mix of the coaching system, and each of us as a coach has our own system, our own dynamic, which is ever moving and changing. When considering how we are doing today, it is up to us to ponder whether we are fit to practice. In between completing my own doctoral research and writing this book, significant trauma hit our lives through the sudden, premature, and unexpected death of the closest and dearest of life-long friends – her name was Julie. The impact and magnitude of losing her are beyond words.

I am sharing my own vulnerability here with you, as it is important to acknowledge that trauma happens in our lives as practitioners; we are not immune to it. When it hits, we must acknowledge it and move into self-care mode, both for ourselves and also for our clients. It is our duty of care to ourselves and others. During this period when we lost Julie, I removed myself from practice, as I was not in a place where I could be present, where I was emotionally or mentally well enough to work on a human level with other people. Now some may say that throwing oneself into work can help as a distraction, and that might be a strategy for dealing with loss or trauma. I've seen many leaders do just that. Yet, as coaches, mentors, and supervisors, we are different, as we are in the privileged position of working with other human beings, not merely numbers or widget creation, or whatever it might be. We must put our own oxygen mask on first.

Duty of care beyond client, customer, and coach

As we continue to adopt our systemic lens in this chapter, let us afford ourselves a moment of reflection on how our duty of care may stretch further than just to our client and customer but to the wider system, such as the client's family, and even further. An experienced coach, Laura, shared how she saw her duty of care as being not only to her client and customer but to society more widely. Whilst she was there primarily for the client, to support their growth, development, and improved actions, she saw her duty of care extending beyond the client, as the objective was to enable improvement more widely, even though she might never meet those in her client's system.

If as coaches we are working to support and help the client grow, our actions can impact improvement, or not, for those in the client's system. Yet we are reminded that we can't control the actions the client may choose to take. However, there are other factors we must also consider. One coach shared how and where she conducted coaching sessions bore significance to her sense of duty of care to her client's wellbeing and how this extended beyond the client and customer and to their families. This particular coach had a strict policy that she would not conduct a coaching session whilst the client was driving. No matter how much a client might pressure her to conduct a session as they were driving home, being too busy to have a coaching session during working hours, this coach refused. As coach she would remind clients of the impact on their family if, whilst talking to her, they had an insightful moment that took their attention off the road, and they were involved in an accident. She was very clear that her duty of care extended beyond the client and to the client's family. She could not control the client's actions, but she could mitigate risk by enforcing control on not allowing a coaching session to happen whilst the client was driving.

This coach set clear boundaries in her contracting with how and when she would conduct coaching sessions. If those boundaries did not meet the needs of the client, the coach was prepared to say she was not the right coach and would walk away from the business. A further interpretation of enactment of duty of care existed for a different coach with a client who had children and who was trying to 'do it all'. The coach could see the patterns and behaviours the client was demonstrating – staying late at work, not spending time with the family. However, as the coach, she had to be thoughtful about the boundaries and mindful of what was or was not said in a coaching session, as she recognised she could intentionally or unintentionally influence the client.

This is why we must think deeply about our intentions and at what times we say 'no' or suggest an alternative option to a client. As another experienced coach shared, they would absolutely point out potential hazards to the client. This may go against some coach training advice which dictates that the coach must not advise or direct. From my own experience, it's not as straightforward as that. If a client is crashing towards a catastrophe and I can see that, I may be failing them and myself as a coach and a coaching supervisor by not pointing out something. My own moral compass guides me, and we come back to the point of ethical decision making. A question I come back to in these scenarios is 'what is my intent in raising this?' It helps clarifying the reasoning behind an action and helps me ensure my actions are in service of the client, not myself.

There are people in the coaching relationship we will never meet – the children of a client, the spouse or parents, the team and colleagues. What our duty of care to these people entails is for us to consider and reflect on how we adopt caution in some situations where our actions as coaches can influence the client, even when the client's views differ from our own. There will be times our own views differ and our values too. Handling such scenarios is a delicate process. We can help the client talk, if that fits with the focus of the coaching, and help the client work through what they want to do. The client may be bringing many other people into the coaching conversation, metaphorically. We have an indirect duty to them all.

Concluding thoughts

As coaches, we are not coaching the system, an important differentiator. Yet we can adopt a systemic lens and recognise we have a duty of care that extends beyond the traditional confines of merely the client and the customer. Importantly, we have a duty of care to ourselves – we must put our own oxygen masks on first. We must also consider how we may be intentionally or unintentionally impacting the ripple effect in our clients' systems and remain attuned to how we are enacting our duty of care.

As we reach the end of this chapter, allow yourself time to reflect more on the themes presented in relation to how adopting a systemic lens can help us widen our peripheral vision.

Your practice in focus

What has surfaced for you in your own reflection?

What might you do differently, going forward?

What questions might you take to supervision to help further explore these themes?

References

Athanasopoulou, A. and Dopson, S. (2018) 'A systematic review of executive coaching outcomes: Is it the journey or the destination that matters the most?', *The Leadership Quarterly*, 29(1), pp. 70–88. https://doi.org/10.1016/j.leaqua.2017.11.004

Bachkirova, T. (2016) 'The self of the coach: Conceptualization, issues, and opportunities for practitioner development', *Consulting Psychology Journal: Practice and Research*, 68(2), pp. 143–156. https://doi.org/10.1037/cpb0000055

Hawkins, P. and Turner, E. (2019) *Systemic coaching: Delivering value beyond the individual*. London: Routledge Taylor & Francis Group. doi.org/10.1037/1061-4087.55.2.94

Kramer, A. (2003) 'Proximity as principles: Directness, community norms and the tort of negligence', *Tort Law Review*, 11, pp. 70–103.

Lawrence, P. (2021) *Coaching systemically: Five ways of thinking about systems*. London: Routledge Taylor & Francis Group (Essential coaching skills and knowledge). https://doi.org/10.4324/9780429356001

Louis, D. and Fatien Diochon, P. (2014) 'Educating coaches to power dynamics: Managing multiple agendas within the triangular relationship', *Journal of Psychological Issues in Organizational Culture*, 5(2), pp. 31–47. https://doi.org/10.1002/jpoc.21140

Mayhead, B. (2022) 'Duty of care in coaching: From ethical frameworks to the development of the coach', Doctoral thesis. Oxford Brookes University. https://doi.org/10.24384/sjmq-9b67

Mayhead, B. (2023) 'The systemic nature of duty of care in coaching: Coach, client, customer and beyond', *International Journal of Evidence Based Coaching & Mentoring*, 17. https://doi.org/10.24384/48c3-0x53

O'Connor, S. and Cavanagh, M. (2013) 'The coaching ripple effect: The effects of developmental coaching on wellbeing across organisational networks', *Psychology of Well-Being: Theory, Research and Practice*, 3(1), pp. 1–23. https://doi.org/10.1186/2211-1522-3-2

Pandolfi, C. (2020) 'Active ingredients in executive coaching: A systematic literature review', *International Coaching Psychology Review*, 15(2), pp. 6–30. https://doi.org/10.53841/bpsicpr.2020.15.2.6

Schermuly, C. and Graßmann, C. (2019) 'A literature review on negative effects of coaching – what we know and what we need to know', *Coaching: An International Journal of Theory, Research and Practice*, 12(1), pp. 39–66. https://doi.org/10.1080/17521882.2018.1528621

Whittington, J. (2020) *Systemic coaching and constellations: The principles, practices and application for individuals, teams and groups*. UK: Kogan Page Publishers.

8 Coaching supervision

Navigating the rifts and tensions

Introduction

Welcome to Chapter 8. Up to this point we have explored the meaning of duty of care and developing our understanding of it – how it is up to us as coaches to set and maintain the standards and boundaries. We have delved into the art of contracting, a separate part of our work from written terms of engagement. We also considered endings in coaching relationships before the previous chapter, where I invited you to don a systemic lens in relation to our duty of care. This chapter focuses our attention on supervision, our need for reflexivity and reflective dialogue, and navigating the rifts and tensions we might experience as practitioners.

In our dynamic and complex world of coaching, we understand how a coach's role can be to support a client's growth, help the client gain clarity and insight, and work with the client to develop skills, strategies, and tools for dealing with the issues or work they are focusing on. Our roles are complex, and since each coaching assignment is unique, we frequently find ourselves encountering nuanced rifts – tensions that can challenge the balance between objectivity and empathy, authority and collaboration – and, crucially, the sometimes desired aspiration toward neutrality. In this chapter we will dig into some of these tensions and examine the essential need for supervision to help develop reflexivity and how adopting reflective dialogue is vital for coaches when navigating these challenges.

Coaching is deeply relational (de Haan and Gannon, 2017), with the potential for subjective perspectives, biases, and unintended influences creeping in. Coaches are rarely fully neutral, and whilst they may strive to be, maintaining this stance can prove trickier than it may seem at first. For practitioners, being able to turn to supervision is paramount. Coaching supervision provides a structured, supportive environment where coaches can explore the subtleties of their own responses, behaviours, biases, and blind spots. The space enables coaches to dive deeper into how they are

DOI: 10.4324/9781003502494-9

demonstrating their duty of care to their clients and to themselves as coaches. It offers a reflexive space where the rifts coaches might be experiencing are acknowledged rather than ignored and where the tensions are uncovered and explored, thus allowing for a greater understanding of the dynamics at play.

Reflective dialogue, particularly with a coach supervisor, can enable coaches to see themselves more clearly. It is in these exchanges that a coach can unpack their instinctive reactions, the emotional pulls they might be experiencing, and internal conflicts around interactions in coaching relationships. By addressing these layers through reflective dialogue, coaches can begin to move toward greater self-awareness, gaining the insights to help their understanding of themselves as practitioners.

This chapter will explore the dimensions of supervision, reflexivity, and reflective dialogue, exploring their impact on a coach's ability to hold space for clients authentically and without unnecessary interference. We will examine how coaches can use these practices not only to resolve internal tensions but also to build confidence in the face of the inevitable challenges that arise in their work. In doing so, we'll explore the nuances of whether we should, in fact, relinquish the idea of neutrality and offer pathways for coaches to approach their roles with renewed clarity and purpose.

Coaching supervision and reflective dialogue

Let's start by exploring the meaning of coaching supervision and reflective dialogue. I will be using the terms coaching supervision and supervision interchangeably from now on. There is great complexity in coaching supervision, and it has not yet been empirically defined. Nonetheless, perhaps we can start by accepting coaching supervision's main functions as supporting the growth and skill development of the coach, creating a safe and reflective environment for the coach to process their client–work experiences, and promoting adherence to professional quality, ethical standards, and best practices (Bachkirova, Jackson and Clutterbuck, 2021). Coaching supervision is widely recognised and practised among coaches in Europe, with particularly strong adoption in the United Kingdom. If you are from outside Europe and perhaps not so familiar with coaching supervision, do read on and allow some thinking on whether this might be something you'd like to build into your coaching practice.

In addition to supporting the growth and skill development of the coach, coaching supervision also attends to the emotions of the coach (the supervisee) to help with how they might be affected by the emotions of the client (Lawrence and Whyte, 2014). My own research revealed that coaches' sensemaking of duty of care and their experiences of emotions such as worry and guilt, which they would bring to supervision for reflection, were very closely connected to their own emotions and feelings.

Since coaching supervision is concerned with developing and providing a supportive space, encouraging professional process, and tending to the emotions of the coach, it is positioned fundamentally as a reflective practice that takes place with another person, or persons (Bachkirova and Borrington, 2019; Lawrence, 2021). This reflective practice can be with a paid coach supervisor, a trusted colleague, or a group of colleagues (Lawrence, 2021). Reflection involves periodically stepping back to consider meaning through a dialectical relationship of reflection and action, thus requiring an active application of concepts in practice (Gray, 2007). The application of concepts points to action beyond the supervision conversation or reflective practice, thus the enactment of what has been made sense of in the reflection.

In my own research it was noticeable how the coaches reflected on matters of duty of care with another person, or group of people, in support of the literature on this very point of purpose and enactment. Reflective practice can of course happen alone, through journalling, taking time to reflect by oneself. However, reflective dialogue is different, and this is where we will be focusing our attention in this chapter. Reflective dialogue happens with another person or persons; it is the exchange of dialogue that helps the coach make sense of complex situations and, in the context of this book, of their duty of care, thus moving the coach forward in their thinking and practice.

Reflection as a form of learning is a foundational stone of activity in coaching (Bachkirova and Borrington, 2019) and has the essential ingredients of a meaning-making process aimed to move the practitioner to deeper understanding. Reflection can be systematic, requiring attitudes that value the growth of another, and it can happen with others, that is, an interaction in community (Bachkirova and Borrington, 2019). In my own research, how coaches valued that interaction in community with their supervisor or their peers was hugely significant. On a practical level, supervision acts as a reflective parallel process, allowing the coach, with the guidance of a supervisor, to examine and gain insights through reflective dialogue into the relational dynamics within their coaching interactions (Hawkins, 2016).

The relational systems we work in are non-linear but complex, and as coaches we are often working in dynamic environments with multiple stakeholders. Often the questions of complexity are brought to supervision (Bachkirova et al., 2021). My own research confirmed this sense of complexity in the coach and client relationships and found reflective dialogue was the primary activity coaches turned to. Indeed, the very action of taking part in the interviews for the research was a reflective dialogue experience for the coaches as they made sense of duty of care for themselves. For most, it was the first time they'd thought deeply about it.

Requirement, or not, to engage in coaching supervision

Speaking from my own experience, having coaching supervision is a vital ingredient in my work. Regular coaching supervision provides me with a space for reflection, skill development, and at times also emotional support. It also offers me ethical guidance, accountability, and an objective perspective, all of which contribute to improved outcomes for my clients and help ensure I'm operating ethically.

Aside from my own personal experience, coaches in my research shared how reflective dialogue with their supervisors was part of their sensemaking and enactment of their duty of care and their preferred option when faced with an ethical dilemma (Mayhead, 2022). Reflective dialogue through supervision is an essential component of how coaches make sense of ethical matters in their practice, supporting their continued development in relation to ethics (Carroll and Shaw, 2013, Mayhead, 2022).

It was evident from my research how supervision was taken seriously by coaches and not viewed as a tick-box exercise. Notably, and in support of the literature on the value of supervision, most of the interviewed coaches reverted to reflective dialogue with their supervisors on concerns relating to duty of care and ethical dilemmas (Hawkins, 2016; Lawrence, 2021). Yet a review of the requirements of the leading coaching bodies for coaches to engage in coaching supervision reveals disparity. The EMCC requires accredited coaches to have 1 hour of coaching supervision for each 35 hours of coaching practice (https://www.emccglobal.org). The Association for Coaching stipulates a 'foundation coach' must have 1 hour's supervision for 15 hours' coaching practice, and 'master coaches' must have 1 hour supervision for 40 hours of coaching practice (https://www.associationforcoaching.com). Might we assume that the Association for Coaching considers that the more experience a coach has, the less supervision they need?

The International Coach Federation states that a credentialled coach may use up to ten hours of coach mentoring (receiving or delivering) to meet the Continuing Coach Education requirements for credential renewal, yet only very recently have they introduced coaching supervision requirements for coaches (https://coachingfederation.org). The ICF is a global organisation but is based in the US, which may be an indicator of why the term 'coach mentoring' was used previously and not 'coach supervision', as supervision as a term has legal connotations in the US (Lawrence, 2021). APECS states that accredited coaches must provide evidence of and commitment to continuing personal professional development, including self-awareness and supervision, but does not stipulate the number of hours required.

Coaching has drawn on related helping professions to form its ethical codes of practice and standards (Iordanou, Hawley and Iordanou, 2017), yet required supervision hours from coaching bodies are low compared to related professions such as counselling and psychotherapy. Although it is acknowledged that coaching is not the same as counselling and psychotherapy, these related helping professions require their therapists to have supervision as a matter of course, not only when in crisis. The British Association for Counselling and Psychotherapy (BACP) stipulates a member must have at least 1.5 hours of supervision per calendar month, regardless of the number of contracted hours being worked. This approach results in the therapist having supervision, regardless of case load, or whether they are in crisis. As we have already discussed, coaching is complex, and a coach could be working with scores of clients before engaging in supervision if following the EMCC requirements, for example, or could have sporadic supervision, or only when in crisis.

As highlighted, there is disparity in how, unlike in counselling and psychotherapy, coaching bodies require, or do not require, supervision to be an integral part of a coach's practice. Coaches rely on supervision as their main source of reflection and support on matters pertaining to duty of care and ethical dilemmas. Furthermore, there is an implied assumption that the more experienced a coach is, the less supervision is needed. My own research found that as coaches matured in their practice, their need for supervision increased (Mayhead, 2022). Supervision remained or grew in level of importance and regularity as an integral part of the coaches' reflective practice. This highlights how coaches value supervision and the learning they derive from it, as well as how their appreciation and learning evolves over time (Sheppard, 2017). Coaches gain multiple layers of perspective through reflection in supervision, and they have supervision regardless of it being a professional requirement (Sheppard, 2017). This demonstrates how supervision has an integral part in how coaches make sense of their role and their duty of care and goes beyond simply meeting a professional requirement (Mayhead, 2022).

Another point to highlight is how coaches turn to reflective dialogue in supervision in times of ethical dilemmas or conflicts, regardless of whether they are a member of a coaching body (Mayhead, 2022). Coaches can experience tensions in their practice and these tensions often relate to boundaries in coaching engagements. It is suggested that 'responsible' coaches engage in constant development and question their own capabilities and conduct through reflective practice and supervision (Hawkins, 2016; Carroll, 2018). However, the literature does not tell us the percentage of coaches who do, nor can we ever obtain reliable representative data of all practitioners in a non-regulated industry. Nevertheless, coaches are responsible for deciding how they operate and whether to engage in developmental learning practices, such as supervision. Building on the premise that the coach is the main instrument in coaching (Bachkirova, 2016), skills and competence alone do not suffice; rather, a coach's ethics, performance, and professionalism are needed to ensure good practice (Jackson and Bachkirova, 2018).

As we touched on early in the book, whilst coaches might follow ethical codes, they are unlikely to rely on them at times when ethical conflicts arise but instead will revert to dialogue with supervisors or peers (Mayhead, 2022). On the one hand, ethical codes serve as a guide for coaches, yet on the other hand, acceptance of or reliance on the codes as the full answer to a problem could be naïve (Mayhead, 2022). Instead, the grey areas experienced in coaching assignments are discussed with peers and supervisors in conversation.

In summary, the need for supervision grows and does not diminish as the coach becomes more experienced, and coaches use supervision as their main resource when managing ethical dilemmas, and for sensemaking in their day-to-day practices as coaches (Mayhead, 2022). This challenges coaching bodies who adopt the position that the more experienced a coach is, the less need there is for supervision. There is an opportunity here for coaching bodies to review their requirement levels for supervision, in line with other helping professions, and an opportunity for coaches who are not part of a coaching body to adopt supervision as part of their practice, not only when they are faced with an ethical dilemma, if they do not do so already (Mayhead, 2022). Coaching supervision can become part of the fabric of coaches' education and development (Mayhead, 2022).

Navigating the rifts

We discussed in the previous chapter how adopting a systemic lens can help us widen our peripheral vision on where our duty of care lies in relation to the ever moving dynamic of the coaching relationship. It is our responsibility as coaches to ensure we clearly understand to whom we have a duty of care and to evaluate how we will enact our duty of care to ensure the avoidance of harm.

When coaching is running smoothly, it can feel collaborative, with progress being made, and perhaps values aligned between the coach and client. However, even in the most established coaching partnerships, there can be situations where challenges arise. These situations, be they misunder-standings, unmet expectations, oversight of assumptions, conflicting per-spectives, or boundaries becoming blurred, can create rifts in the coaching relationship.

When rifts occur, as they inevitably will, it is essential we recognise and address them to avoid breakdowns in trust and communication, or worse. We can experience tension when finding ourselves in challenging power dynamics, when boundaries are being crossed, or when we are feeling com-promised. Acknowledging and working through rifts is an opportunity for growth, yet can also feel uncomfortable. If we accept that our duty of care stretches beyond the confines of the coach and client relationship to the customer and more broadly, this challenges us to reflect on our perceived neutrality as coaches.

In this next section we will explore the rifts we may experience in rela-tion to our neutrality as coaches, what happens when we find ourselves caught up in the tensions, and the role coaching supervision and reflective dialogue can play in navigating us through. Experiences from coaches will be shared to illustrate these points, and I invite you to reflect, as you read, on your own practice and when there have been times you might have expe-rienced similar rifts.

Neutrality – achievable or an outdated narrative?

The very title of this section gives a clue as to where we might be going with the discussion on neutrality. Neutrality has long been a lauded and desired competency of coaches (Carey, Philippon and Cummings, 2011; Cushion, 2018). Yet in situations characterised by inequality or oppression, it is impractical and sometimes even unethical for coaches to maintain com-plete neutrality (Shoukry and Cox, 2018). The notion that coaches are neu-tral is challenged if, outside of social contexts of inequality or oppression, a coach sees their duty of care as being primarily for one party or another in the coaching relationship. Despite this, they still might strive to create the appearance of neutrality (Pliopas, 2017). The reality is that coaches are often engaged in complex triangular relationships prone to ethical dilemmas and conflicts of interest (Pliopas, 2017; Louis and Fatien Diochon, 2019). Indeed, there has been critique on the lack of empirical understanding of neutrality in coaching, with it being an often-emphasised but less explored standard for coaches (Fatien Diochon, Louis and Islam, 2022).

This brings us to the question of whether neutrality is achievable or whether striving towards it is an outdated narrative. As a practitioner and coach supervisor, I have frequently heard coaches say how they are neutral, yet when we stop to interrogate their reasoning, what are they actually claiming? Some coaches believe they demonstrate their neutrality by not sharing their own perspective or experiences. Yet this approach might impact the coach's ability to be honest. Let me give some examples to illustrate this.

One coach shared with me how he considered himself neutral and how he believed he should not have any objectives when coaching. He explained how he felt his duty involved not having an objective for his clients, but he also found it difficult to put his own desires and wants for the client's success to one side, and this was further compounded when he cared about the person. Other coaches were clear in not seeing themselves as purely neutral agents. In contrast, some demonstrated their duty of care through sharing their experiences when they perceived it to be useful to the client.

Another coach explained how their experience of having walked in the shoes of the client or sat in the chair the client was in were helpful reference points. In this example, the coach saw it as her duty to use those experiences and reference points in ways that were helpful to the client, yet she also recognised how this diverged from some coaching body competencies which stipulate that the coach must not guide the client (Mayhead, 2022).

These are several positions of how coaches see neutrality in their roles, from one extreme of remaining without objectives to the other of actively bringing experiences into the coaching dynamic if helpful to the client. Let's consider an alternative perspective: the coach who considered their duty of care to themselves and to their clients was demonstrated by occasionally alerting clients if they saw them heading towards a catastrophe. They would be directive in those situations and would point out the disaster ahead. Pointing to a potential hazard was done when useful, with the coach not setting the goal or direction but working to the client's needs (Mayhead, 2022).

In this example, the coach might point out future problems and help the client catch themselves before they sank, but there were situations where coaches enacted their duty of care in completely the opposite way. One coach would leave their client 'in a mess', as she described it, for a while, affording the client time to work out what to do. For this coach, her duty of care was not to warn or act but to step back.

There is a balance in how we understand the needs of our clients and when we recognise that it might be best to help them out of the 'mess', but an alternative might be to leave them in it. We must seek to understand what it is we are doing as coaches and recognise the balance between caring and realising that caring can also be helping the client hold themselves accountable. It is up to us to reflect on our own practice and evaluate our intentions, actions, and neutrality. Whilst coaches might talk of being neutral, of being an independent party, my research found that it was not as simple as that. This leads to a question for coaches to challenge their own practice in how they manage perceived neutrality with their clients and whether neutrality is even achievable (Mayhead, 2022).

Tensions

It is inevitable in our work as coaches that we will experience tensions in coaching relationships. Often described as ethical dilemmas, these are situations where the available options and responsibilities make it challenging to achieve an entirely ethical outcome, often forcing a choice that goes against a specific ethical principle or standard we might hold as coaches. The dilemmas can arise when dealing with people who have differing moral beliefs or ethical responsibilities or when we are balancing multiple roles with conflicting obligations. They can manifest in a variety of scenarios, such as matters involving a choice between personal integrity and loyalty, prioritising individual interests versus the greater good, weighing immediate gains against future outcomes, or balancing fairness in consequences with the need for compassion (Turvey and Crowder, 2013).

It is worth noting that, in our roles as coaches, ethical dilemmas are practically inevitable when collaborating with individuals who have differing beliefs or ethical responsibilities or when fulfilling multiple roles with varying obligations. We can't avoid them, unfortunately, and if a coach is not experiencing any, as those situations are potentially going unnoticed, this raises the question – what might they be missing and where are their blind spots? This is a dangerous position for the coach and the client to be in. When we find ourselves faced with an ethical dilemma, we can experience tensions in ourselves, between the parties involved, and between our own beliefs and values. Engaging in coaching supervision and reflective dialogue is key to helping us unlock our thinking here.

Let's consider some tensions often experienced by coaches. In the case of executive coaching, for example, it is often expected that strict confidentiality be maintained in managing relationships with clients whilst also fulfilling the requests of those who are funding the coaching process (Pichault, Diochon and Nizet, 2020). This can be a conflicting situation for coaches to be in, as my own research also found (Mayhead, 2022). An executive coach in my research shared how they found it challenging when a client they were coaching decided to leave the organisation whilst they were in a coaching engagement. The coach believed that their client was their priority of focus, and if the best outcome from the coaching process was for the client to leave the company, then so be it.

The coach experienced the pressure of not wanting to be seen as complicit in or encouraging the client's departure. Whilst she did not believe the coaching was the catalyst for the client's decision to leave, at the same time she was left with the ethical dilemma of what to do. Her navigation of this was done through her self-reflection and decision making on choices of actions she might take, and she took her reflections to coaching supervision. She questioned with her coach supervisor whether her duty of care was to support the client in that move or to the client's organisation and whether she should guide the client not to move. In this scenario, the coach was pulled between either 'betraying the customer, or the client', as she put it. As the reader, what are your thoughts on this? What would you have done?

If we turn our attention back to our earlier chapter on contracting, we can remind ourselves of the importance of setting clear boundaries at the very start of a coaching assignment. In this shared example of the client expressing a desire to leave the organisation, had the coach set clear boundaries at the start, they may not have experienced such tension. That's not to say the issue wouldn't have arisen, but the coach may have signalled to the client at the start that potential issues of conflict might arise if the coach was perceived to be colluding with the client. In practice, I have experienced this exact scenario. I re-contract with the client when it happens and agree what will be in and out of scope with the coaching.

Coaches also experience political challenges in their navigation in organisations with how they manage the sensitivities of key stakeholder needs. One coach shared how he found it frustrating when the HR department checked in with him, wanting to know how the coaching was going. This is perhaps not an unreasonable request when an organisation has commissioned coaching work, but boundaries need to be set in the contracting stage. This coach took the dilemma to coaching supervision. Again, if we can return to clear boundaries, the coach and the organisation can agree upfront what is going to be fed back to the organisation and how. This can help alleviate tensions, yet, as in the previous example, this doesn't necessarily stop the coach feeling compromised. There are times when a key stakeholder may ask the coach to breach confidentiality, to provide further information on the coaching than had been agreed upon.

Let's explore this a bit further. Take the example of a coach who had been given complete autonomy with a client, enabling the client's return to work after a period of absence. Whilst the coach was given complete autonomy, they shared how they experienced tension when the organisation probed and asking for information. In this scenario, the coach had to navigate with care and sensitivity, using coaching supervision to help them work through a plan of how to go back to the contracting and what was agreed upon, and how to maintain the trust of the client in the coaching process, thus enabling their continued ability to focus on their return-to-work plan.

Organisations frequently ask coaches to break confidentiality, to provide information. Coaches described how they deflect this issue early on in coaching relationships through contracting for what would and would not be shared (Mayhead, 2022). Even so, it happens, unlike in professions such as psychotherapy where it is more commonly accepted that nothing will be shared. In coaching, there can be an expectation from stakeholders in the coaching relationship that the coach will divulge certain information or progress, which is not typically the case in fields like psychotherapy, where strict confidentiality is the norm. This creates a unique dynamic in coaching, where balancing transparency with confidentiality becomes a crucial aspect of the coach's practice.

Permission is central in the coaching relationship, which establishes what will be communicated and what will not. Gaining permission is especially important when coaches are working with an entire leadership team, for example. The coach must be mindful of how they reveal knowledge gained without breaking confidentiality. This is a privileged position for the coach to be in, with the coach having greater insight than most into the overall dynamics of the team. If they have not clearly contracted in the beginning, coaches can find themselves experiencing tension with how to serve the organisation, the team, and the individual (Mayhead, 2022).

The internal coach also experiences tensions which are often related to managing the boundaries between work and personal issues (St John Brooks, 2018). Most often, the internal coach works in a capacity of support to employees and on behalf of the organisation. Whilst boundaries of confidentiality may be in place, the internal coach does not escape ethical dilemmas, for instance, of a senior figurehead pressuring them to divulge information and break confidentiality or the tension of hearing something about another employee that may not sit well with them. Coaching supervision is also crucial to the internal coach.

The internal coach acts as a vessel, and they hold information and knowledge of others in the business and need to develop the ability to be comfortable with this and to retain objectivity. Contracting, boundary setting, confidentiality, and support in how to deal with power differentials are crucial components of the process, as are providing support through a senior internal coach and coaching supervision. Organisations with clear process, structure, and support for their internal programmes fare better. Once again, we can see how supervision plays a vital part in the support structure for the internal coach.

Our own oxygen mask first

Coaching supervision not only enables the development and growth of the coach and the untangling of ethical dilemmas and situations but also acts as a restorative function for the coach. Matters of legal issues, accusations of misconduct, unprofessional or unethical behaviour, conflicts of interest regardless of whether correct can lead to significant stress for the coach. A coach supervisor can provide emotional and mental support and help the coach navigate through (Bachkirova et al., 2021). Furthermore, it might be prudent for the coach to work with a supervisor by way of evidencing that they have taken measures to fulfil their duty of care (Bachkirova et al., 2021), should a claim be brought against the coach. This may seem alarming, and my aim is not to put fear into practitioners, yet we must be alert. Additionally, there are less serious matters which can still leave a coach feeling overburdened, experiencing the emotional and mental strain that can cause anxiety. Again, coaching supervision can provide a restorative function for the coach.

Widely acknowledged across the coaches in my research was how duty of care extended also to themselves as coaches. Coaches talked of putting their own oxygen mask on first – the analogy used in aircraft safety briefings where passengers are told to tend to their own need for oxygen before helping others. Coaches have a need to ensure that they themselves are in a good state to practice (Mayhead, 2022). One coach shared how he would check in with himself to ensure he wasn't under threat, as he described it, that he wasn't feeling stressed and was able to deal with any dilemmas that might face him (Mayhead, 2022).

I've said many times in this book how coaching is complex, with role boundaries not always clearly defined. As a coach, deciding what is in and out of our area of expertise is arguably more accessible when we are free from stress or threat ourselves (Mayhead, 2022). Maintaining boundaries and remaining safe are more difficult to achieve otherwise. Engaging in supervision around how to help ourselves to put our own oxygen masks on first is needed. Coaches can find they focus outwardly on their clients and their customers but less so on themselves (Mayhead, 2022). As I shared in the previous chapter, when we experience a significant trauma, such as bereavement, we have a duty of care to ourselves and our clients to remove ourselves from our work so we can heal and recover until we are fit to practice.

Coaching supervision was discussed previously as a sense-making mechanism for coaches, and it also relates to how coaches enact their duty of care. It is used as a way for coaches to become sensitised to the duty of care they have for themselves and how they recognise whether they are actively present in coaching sessions (Mayhead, 2022). One coach explained how she enacted care for herself through being cognisant of what she experienced in a coaching session. She achieved this through constant listening to how she was feeling in herself, consciously noticing how she was physically, having gratitude to herself and questioning what she needed to do differently to keep herself alert and present. She explained how she couldn't be a good coach if she wasn't listening to herself (Mayhead, 2022). Perhaps this is unsurprising to you as you read this, and perhaps in your practice you do place your own duty of care to yourself in the centre. Or perhaps you are realising there is an opportunity for you to do more for yourself.

Concluding thoughts

Tensions are inevitable, as are ethical dilemmas and challenging situations surrounding perceived neutrality. Coaching supervision is a requirement for some coaching bodies, but it is a practice yet to be adopted more widely across geographies outside of Europe. Engaging in reflective dialogue with a coach supervisor is an enabler for the coach to tend to areas of concern, to continue to develop and grow in their practice.

Coaching can be a lonely place, and engaging in supervision can be a powerful support mechanism, providing a restorative function. It can also serve as evidence for a coach to be able to demonstrate they have taken steps to exercise their duty of care.

As we reach the end of this chapter, I pose some questions for you.

Your practice in focus

What are your thoughts on your own practices of stepping back and giving space for reflective dialogue with a coach supervisor?

Are you putting your own oxygen mask on first?

If you are not engaging in coaching supervision, why is that and would you like to?

What are your views on a coach's perceived neutrality in coaching?

What rifts have you noticed in your coaching experience?

What types of tensions have you experienced?

References

Bachkirova, T. (2016) 'The self of the coach: Conceptualization, issues, and opportunities for practitioner development', *Consulting Psychology Journal: Practice and Research*, 68(2), pp. 143–156. https://doi.org/10.1037/cpb0000055

Bachkirova, T. and Borrington S. (2019) 'Old wine in new bottles: Exploring pragmatism as a philosophical framework for the discipline of coaching,' *Academy of Management Learning and Education*, 18(3), pp. 337–360. https://doi.org/10.5465/amle.2017.0268

Bachkirova, T., Jackson, P. and Clutterbuck, D. (2021) *Coaching and Mentoring Supervision: Theory and Practice.* 2nd Ed. UK: McGraw-Hill Education.

Carey, W., Philippon, D. and Cummings, G. (2011) 'Coaching models for leadership development: An integrative review', *Journal of Leadership Studies*, 5(1), 51–69. https://doi.org/10.1002/jls.20204

Carroll, M. (2018) 'Coaching psychology supervision: Luxury or necessity?' In *Handbook of coaching psychology: A guide for practitioners*, eds. S. Palmer and A. Whybrow. Routledge. pp. 431–448.

Carroll, M. and Shaw, E. (2013) *Ethical maturity in the helping professions: Making difficult life and work decisions.* UK: Jessica Kingsley Publishers.

Cushion, C.J. (2018) 'Reflection and reflective practice discourses in coaching: A critical analysis', *Sport, Education and Society*, 23(1), pp. 82–94. https://doi.org/10.1080/13573322.2016.1142961

De Haan, E. and Gannon, J. (2017) 'The coaching relationship', In *The SAGE handbook of coaching.* London: SAGE. pp. 195–217.

Fatien Diochon, P., Louis, D. and Islam, G. (2022) 'Neutral in-tensions: Navigating neutrality in coaching', *Journal of Management Studies*. https://doi.org/10.1111/joms.12883

Gray, D.E. (2007) 'Facilitating management learning: Developing critical reflection through reflective tools', *Management Learning*, 38(5), pp. 495–517. https://doi.org/10.1177/1350507607083204

Hawkins, P. (2016) 'Coaching supervision', In *Excellence in coaching: The industry guide.* Kogan Page Publishers. pp. 257–272.

Iordanou, I., Hawley, R. and Iordanou, C. (2017) *Values and ethics in coaching.* London: Sage. https://doi.org/10.4135/9781473983755

Jackson, P. and Bachkirova, T. (2018) 'The 3Ps of supervision and coaching: Philosophy, purpose and process', In *The heart of coaching supervision. Working with reflection and self-care.* Abingdon: Routledge. pp. 20–40.

Lawrence, P. (2021) *Coaching systemically: Five ways of thinking about systems.* London: Routledge/Taylor & Francis Group (Essential coaching skills and knowledge). https://doi.org/10.4324/9780429356001

Lawrence, P. and Whyte, A. (2014) 'What is coaching supervision and is it important?', *Coaching: An International Journal of Theory, Research and Practice*, 7(1), pp. 39–55. https://doi.org/10.1080/17521882.2013.878370

Louis, D. and Fatien Diochon, P. (2019) *Complex situations in coaching: A critical case-based approach.* Routledge. https://doi.org/10.4324/9780429056185

Mayhead, B. (2022) 'Duty of care in coaching: From ethical frameworks to the development of the coach', Doctoral thesis. Oxford Brookes University. https://doi.org/10.24384/sjmq-9b67

Pichault, F., Diochon, P.F. and Nizet, J. (2020) 'Autonomy of independent professionals: A political process perspective', *European Management Journal*, 38(4), pp. 623–633. https://doi.org/10.1016/j.emj.2019.12.007

Pliopas, A. (2017) 'Drawing the triangle: How coaches manage ambiguities inherited in executive coaching?', *BAR Brazilian Administration Review*, 14(4). https://doi.org/10.1590/1807-7692bar2017170050

Sheppard, L. (2017) 'How coaching supervisees help and hinder their supervision', *International Journal of Evidence Based Coaching & Mentoring*, 15.

Shoukry, H. and Cox, E. (2018) 'Coaching as a social process', *Management Learning*, 49(4), pp. 413–428. https://doi.org/10.1177/1350507618762600

St John-Brooks, K. (2018) *Internal coaching: The inside story*. UK: Routledge Taylor and Francis Group. https://doi.org/10.4324/9780429476068

Turvey, B.E. and Crowder, S. (2013) *Ethical justice: Applied issues for criminal justice students and professionals*. Academic Press.

9 Bringing it together

Putting good practice in to practice

Introduction

This penultimate chapter provides an opportunity to reflect and engage further in thinking about the topics and themes covered in the book. A brief summary of each chapter is offered, with questions for you as the reader to contemplate. My aim is to give you a snapshot of the book in one place so you can refer back to the individual chapters for more in-depth discussion.

Let's start at the beginning of the book, where, in the Introduction, attention was drawn to a consideration of individual contexts and to the uniqueness of cultural difference, as well as how the practitioner needs awareness of legal requirements in their common law jurisdiction. As we consider what duty of care means to us and how we enact it in our roles as practitioners, we are reminded to pay attention to these points.

As this book attests, it is helpful for us to develop appreciation of the complexity of duty of care and to broaden our understanding of its importance in practice. Duty of care forms part of the ethical framework of conduct for a practitioner, whether they are a coach, mentor, or coaching supervisor. It is associated with the practitioner's sense of fairness, of right and wrong, both legally and ethically (Iordanou, Hawley and Iordanou, 2017). Coaching bodies have competency frameworks and codes of ethics to guide practitioners, yet these alone do not suffice. Furthermore, not all coaches, mentors, or supervisors are qualified or members of professional bodies. Regardless of qualifications or professional body membership, practitioners are required to uphold the legal requirements of common law jurisdictions.

The multi-faceted nature of duty of care requires our attention and focus on developing a deeper understanding of its meaning and an awareness of how we enact it. It's time for us to polish our mirrors and take a good look at ourselves in relation to the topic. We also have an opportunity to pause as a community and take stock of the current landscape. We run the risk of our field moving further away from its theoretical foundations as coaching grows exponentially in scale, due to technology-enabled platforms and artificial intelligence.

DOI: 10.4324/9781003502494-10

The Introduction offers a suite of questions designed to draw out readers' own meaning making of duty of care and how practitioners enact it. Here is a sample of the questions (do refer back to the chapter for further guidelines on how to approach answering the questions):

What does duty of care mean to you in your role?

What has helped shape and influence your understanding of duty of care?

Who has helped shape and influence your understanding of duty of care?

What is it that you do to demonstrate your duty of care?

How do you continue to develop you own sense of understanding of duty of care?

Duty of care in coaching; shifting sands of change

As discussed in Chapter 1, duty of care in coaching has received little attention in the literature, with paucity in research. Related helping professions, such as psychotherapy and counselling, are further developed in their
understanding of it, as indeed is the domain of sports coaching. Duty of care
encompasses both legal and ethical dimensions and is part of the ethical
framework of conduct. As coaches, mentors, or coaching supervisors, we
have a responsibility to work within the legal requirements of the common
law jurisdictions we are practising in. Although there are no specific laws
in coaching, practitioners are required to adhere to the general law of civil
liability, the common law of tort. Practitioners are also bound by the law of
contract, which applies regardless of whether terms are in writing.

In addition to the legal requirements, duty of care also applies to the ethical and moral elements of practice. Coaches associate duty of care with their
own sense of what is fair and right and draw on life experience and role
models when making sense of what it means to them (Mayhead, 2022). Furthermore, they draw on coaching supervision and reflective dialogue when
finding themselves in ethical dilemmas. It is noteworthy that coaches rarely
draw from training or codes of ethics in such circumstances. Professional
coaching bodies uphold ethical principles and best practice, with codes of
ethics going some way towards guiding us on standards and behaviours.
Yet codes cannot and do not cover all eventualities, and it might be harmful
for coaches to rely purely on a code of ethics when solving ethical problems
(Louis and Fatien Diochon, 2019).

We also discussed in Chapter 1 how the coaching market is growing exponentially and how technology and AI are adding to the changing
landscape – the sands are ever shifting. In our current technology-enabled
world, we are presented with advantages and disadvantages, from ease and
accessibility of working remotely to ethical concerns for coaches being targeted to achieve specific goals when working for some tech-enabled coaching platforms. Conversations on ethical concerns are less prevalent, with
greater focus on demonstrated return on investment. Legislation is in place,
yet the advancement of the field is at such a rate that we are running before
we can walk.

Some questions for reflection, bringing your practice in to focus:

For those abiding by a code of ethics, take some time to interrogate your understanding of the code, reflect on meaning, and how it applies to your practice. Critically reflect on the elements included and challenge your understanding of them and whether you do, or even can, uphold them.

How is technology, including AI, impacting your practice?

What measures have you put in place to safeguard yourself and those in the coaching relationship (including the customer)?

What are your legal and ethical responsibilities in matters of technology and AI?

What is the potential impact of technology or AI on those in the coaching relationship, including yourself?

How are you adhering to relevant regulations, for example, the AI EU Act?

Building understanding of duty of care in coaching

As may be the case with some of the concepts discussed in this book, opinion will be divided. One such concept that I consider will divide opinion is whether we should, or should not, define duty of care in coaching. I appreciate that defining it could portray it too simplistically. However, if we can write down neatly what it means, have we not just missed the point entirely? So, as discussed in this chapter, I invite you to consider the definition a complementary resource, which can support a stronger theoretical understanding of how duty of care is conceptualised and which can help guide us as practitioners.

Coaches draw on their own past experiences and influence from role models when thinking about what duty of care means to them, less so from textbooks, training, or codes of ethics (Mayhead, 2022). How we enact our duty of care includes how we manage boundaries, limits, contracting, and endings. Accounts shared in this chapter illustrate how lived experiences from childhood, family members, teachers, values, and one's own humanity have shaped coaches' life philosophies. These accounts bring to light the complex tapestry of what duty of care means on an individual level. Our ethical maturity continues to develop, as does our self-awareness, and these in turn can inform our practice.

The chapter ends with the definition, accompanied by a note of caution. The definition is offered as a developmental tool – to generate debate and thinking with peers or in supervision, perhaps.

> *Duty of care is an ethical and legal obligation for the coach not to cause harm and forms part of the ethical framework of conduct encompassing the coach's adherence to a standard of reasonable professional care. The coach's responsibility includes setting and maintaining boundaries between ethically acceptable and unacceptable influence on the client, customer, and those in the coaching relationship.*

Some thought-provoking questions from this chapter are built around an interrogation of the definition, a dissection of its elements, and applying it to your own practice. The chapter includes more questions, but a sample of five is included here:

What does an ethical obligation mean to you?

What are your legal obligations?

What does reasonable professional care mean to you?

What ethical framework of conduct do you follow?

How do you establish and maintain the boundaries in your coaching practice?

Boundaries and standards

Part of how a coach enacts their duty of care includes the setting and main-taining of boundaries and upholding ethical and professional standards. The responsibility for setting and maintaining the boundaries and standards requires the coach to operate within the boundaries of their level of expe-rience and skill. Having written agreements of services is recommended, although these can also be verbal.

Conversations on ethical dilemmas brought by coaches to supervision often include the topic of boundaries and how to manage them. Boundaries are complex and include both practical and interpersonal elements, and the boundaries between coaching and therapy can be blurred. Gaining clarity on boundaries between the parties in the coaching relationship at the contract-ing stage is a vital step. There is growing awareness of the critical role men-tal health plays, and coaches must recognise when a client's needs extend beyond the limits of the coach's capability.

Standards establish the expected level of competence and ethical respon-sibilities coaches are to uphold. This also has particular relevance to the level at which a coach may market themselves. For example, a Master Cer-tified Coach has a duty to deliver a standard at a particular level, which differs from that of a coach who is an Associate. Our awareness starts with us – knowing ourselves, recognising biases, emotions, and intentions.

Some questions for reflection, bringing your practice in to focus:

What boundaries do I set in my practice?

How do I maintain those boundaries?

What example do I have of when boundaries have been crossed or have been unclear, and what were the consequences to me and to those in the coaching relationship?

What standards to I adhere to?

Contracting as a coach

Perhaps this is one of the most essential elements of the coaching process, as so much can go wrong if we don't pay attention to it, both at the start and through coaching assignments. Whether conversational in nature or in writing, or indeed a combination of the two, the art of contracting paves the way for how the parties in the coaching relationship intend to work. How coaches contract can differ, with some doing it as a separate conversation, and some bolting it onto the start of the first coaching session.

Contracting is concerned with the formal agreement about services and also with the subtleties of expectation of all parties in the coaching relationship. It also includes the psychological contract. There is no mandate on how coaches should contract, which perhaps explains why we see such a difference in approaches. It is up to us individually to establish how we do it, and we must also understand our own level of capability and expertise. There may be times when coaching moves beyond the coach's capability, and this can be signposted during contracting.

Contracting can include the roles and responsibilities of those in the coaching relationship, how confidentiality will be managed, what access the client and customer will have to the coach, agreement on where and when the coaching will take place, and endings and letting go. Contracting throughout the coaching process through re-contracting is a valuable practice for the coach, one which supports their enactment of their duty of care.

Some questions for reflection, bringing your practice in to focus:

How do you contract with those in the coaching relationship?

What do your clients and customers understand about contracting? What opportunities are there for you to talk to them about contracting and the need for it?

How do you re-contract?

Reflect back to a situation where you experienced an ethical dilemma in your coaching practice. How could contracting and re-contracting have helped avoid or reduce the impact of the ethical dilemma?

Care and coaching; developing ethical maturity

As we are engaging with fellow human beings in our roles as coaches, our work unsurprisingly brings a level of responsibility to take care in what we do, to work responsibility, and to uphold the law. 'Care' in this context is not to be confused with being responsible for another person or taking care of another, as might be the case for a medical practitioner, for example.

Coaching has become recognised as a way of helping people, and in the last decade we have seen a shift in organisations. As stress levels are on the rise, organisations are increasingly focusing on happiness and wellbeing for employees. We know that episodes of renewal, such as coaching, can help with overall improvement in how people feel. It is crucial for coaches to examine their intent, to recognise potential inherent characteristics of wanting to help others, and to safeguard against potential pitfalls of over-caring or rescuing. My own research also found that coaches experience emotions with their work and a sense of having a 'duty *to* care'. They experience emotional burdens with feelings of worry, and carrying those feelings can be a hazard of the job.

Our own development of ethical maturity is continual and is an indispensable part of our growth to help us navigate complexity in the intricate web of multiple stakeholders in coaching relationships. The flow of development towards ethical maturity is continual – we don't just arrive at ethical maturity; it is not a destination (Carroll and Shaw, 2013). Instead, our development of ethical maturity is not linear, and we oscillate between multiple elements through reflection and honesty about ourselves.

Some questions for reflection, bringing your practice in to focus:

What does having a 'duty to care' mean to you in your role?

What experiences have you had of over-caring in the work you do?

What did you experience, and what was the impact on you as a practitioner?

Chapter 5 (Carroll, 2018) shares five factors integral to developing ethical maturity: demonstrating ethical sensitivity; making discerning ethical decisions; understanding one's own decisions; using reflection honestly; demonstrating self-compassion. Take a moment to consider each of these and what you are experiencing in your development towards ethical maturity.

Endings in coaching

Endings are a natural part of life, sometimes in a positive way, and sometimes more challenging and painful. Endings provide an opportunity for closure and a sense of completion before moving forward. They allow space for the next phase to begin or time for evaluation and celebration. Importantly, endings allow time for pause and reflection. In related helping professions, both therapist and patient can adjust and work towards endings, avoiding an abrupt halt and co-creating a good-enough ending (Salberg, 2009).

In coaching, the relationship between client and coach is different from a clinical relationship between therapist and patient (Cox, 2010). Whilst different, endings still have significance and are important, just as important as beginnings. Who decides when endings happen in coaching is an area sparsely debated in the literature. We can draw on codes of ethics to guide us in when and how to terminate an engagement, in how the duration of the coaching contract is appropriate to the needs of the client (and customer). Yet how coaching ends varies – some coaches act as the decider, others co-create a plan with the client and customer, and of course there are situations when the coaching ends unexpectedly. We have an opportunity as practitioners to co-create how coaching ends with those in the coaching relationship, striving for what is a good-enough ending.

Some questions for reflection, bringing your practice in to focus:

What is my relationship with endings like, and how do my own experiences impact my coaching practice?

What steps am I taking to ensure coaching relationships have meaningful closure?

What is my role in ending coaching, and what is the role of the client and the customer?

How do I consider a client's emotional state and readiness for ending a coaching relationship?

How do I balance my own emotional investment with a need to maintain my own ethical standards when it's time to end coaching relationships?

Adopting a systemic lens

We have the opportunity to build broader awareness of and sensitivity to the systems that influence our coaching practices and the impact we have on those we are working with. By adopting a systemic lens, we can examine our own duty of care from multiple angles and develop understanding of the interconnected forces that shape us and the choices we make.

A typical triangular coaching relationship includes the coach, the client, and the customer. Yet coaches also talk of having a duty of care beyond these three. This might include an organisation they are subcontracted to, the coaching field, the client's personal life and family, society, and more broadly the world. Coaching has influence beyond just the person being coached, and the impact of coaching can be positive or negative. The ripple effect of our work goes beyond what happens in the coaching room, and most of the time, we are unlikely to know the detail of that impact. Yet, it is for us to think about our intention in actions we take as practitioners and to consider to whom we have a duty of care.

We can adopt a systemic lens and recognise we have a duty of care that extends beyond the traditional confines of the client and the customer only. Included in this is how we look after ourselves. By putting our own oxygen masks on first, we can help maintain a duty of care to ourselves.

Some questions for reflection, bringing your practice in to focus:

To whom do you have a duty of care?

What does adopting a systemic lens with duty of care mean to you?

How do you navigate duty of care across multiple stakeholders?

What ripple effects have you been aware of from the work you do as a practitioner?

With regard to a duty of care to yourself, how do you ensure your own oxygen mask is on first?

Coaching supervision; navigating the rifts and tensions

The role of a coach can be complex: each assignment is unique, and we can find ourselves encountering nuanced rifts. Tensions can challenge the balance, and whilst some practitioners may strive to be neutral, it can rarely be truly achieved. Coaching supervision provides a structured and supportive environment where the subtleties of one's own response, practice, behaviours, biases, perceived neutrality, and blind spots can be explored.

Coaching supervision enables coaches to dive further into how they are demonstrating duty of care to those in the coaching relationship. It offers a reflexive space where rifts are acknowledged, rather than ignored; where tensions are brought into the light and explored, thus enabling the coach to achieve greater clarity. Reflection can happen alone, through journalling, and through thinking. As a form of learning, it is a foundational stone of activity in coaching (Bachkirova and Borrington, 2020). Engaging in reflective dialogue with another person, such as a coaching supervisor or peer, enables an exchange which allows us to go further, to step back and consider meaning. These exchanges of dialogue can help coaches make sense of complex situations and of their duty of care.

As the coach grows in experience, the complexity of their case load may also grow. Our need for supervision does not decrease as we mature; it increases (Mayhead, 2022). Ethical dilemmas are practically inevitable, and we can't avoid them. A coach rarely reaches for a code of ethics or a textbook when faced with an ethical dilemma. Instead, they turn to their coaching supervisor (Mayhead, 2022). Coaching supervision not only supports the development and growth of the coach; it also acts as a restorative function. Once again, we are reminded of the importance of putting our own oxygen mask on first.

Some questions for reflection, bringing your practice in to focus:

What are your thoughts on your own practices of working with a coaching supervisor?

Are you putting your own oxygen mask on first?

If you are not engaging in coaching supervision, why is that?

What rifts or tensions have you experienced in your work as a coach?

Concluding thoughts

Duty of care is complex, and we have discussed how we can work on a practical level with the legalities and requirements, and we have also explored how coaches enact it. Rather than seeing duty of care as a checklist, or indeed merely as an obligation, we have the opportunity to integrate it into our thinking, for it to become a mindset and to be woven through all of our work and interactions. As practitioners, we are developing and learning – our ethical maturity develops on a continual cycle and is not a destination we are aiming for.

As you reach the end of the book, I encourage you to reflect on your own strengths and abilities and areas for growth in relation to what has been discussed on the topic of duty of care. We can support and call on each other as practitioners and as a community to be proactive, to be reflective and reflexive and committed to continuous development.

It's a complex role we have, and working with other human beings is a great privilege.

It starts with us.

References

Bachkirova, T. and Borrington S. (2020) 'Old wine in new bottles: Exploring pragmatism as a philosophical framework for the discipline of coaching,' *Academy of Management Learning and Education*, 18(3), pp. 337–360. https://doi.org/10.5465/amle.2017.0268

Carroll, M. (2018) 'Coaching psychology supervision: Luxury or necessity?' In *Handbook of coaching psychology: A guide for practitioners*, eds. S. Palmer and A. Whybrow. Routledge. pp. 431–448.

Carroll, M. and Shaw, E. (2013) *Ethical maturity in the helping professions: Making difficult life and work decisions*. UK: Jessica Kingsley Publishers.

Cox, E. (2010) 'Last things first: Ending well in the coaching relationship', In *The coaching relationship: Putting people first*. London: Taylor & Francis. pp. 159–181.

Iordanou, I., Hawley, R. and Iordanou, C. (2017) *Values and ethics in coaching*. London: Sage. https://doi.org/10.4135/9781473983755

Louis, D. and Diochon, P.F. (2019) *Complex situations in coaching: A critical case-based approach*. Routledge.

Mayhead, B. (2022) 'Duty of care in coaching: From ethical frameworks to the development of the coach', Doctoral thesis. Oxford Brookes University. https://doi.org/10.24384/sjmq-9b67

Salberg, J. (2009) 'Leaning into termination', *Psychoanalytic Dialogues*, 19(6), pp. 704–722.

10 Research overview

Introduction

This next chapter may not be for everyone reading this book, so please bypass it if it's not for you. For those who might be interested, I hope it perhaps helps demystify what goes on at doctoral-level research and helps build confidence in others who may be tempted to take the leap onto this stage of academic qualification. It's important to note that I left school at sixteen and didn't go to university as a young person. But I came to higher education many decades later. I say this to highlight that it's never too late to learn and to push ourselves.

Allow me just a moment to acknowledge a couple of things. The doctorate in coaching and mentoring was honestly one of the best professional experiences of my career. My huge thanks go to the incredible faculty at Oxford Brookes University. I am honoured that Dr Ioanna Iordanou was my director of studies and is now a dear friend. Professor Peter Lugosi was my second supervisor, and as a cohort of students, we had an inspiring team of tutors, including Dr Judie Gannon, Professor Tatiana Bachkirova, Dr Peter Jackson, Dr Adrian Myers, Dr Elaine Cox, Dr Sylwia Ciuk, Dr Joanna Molyn, and Dr Christian Ehrlich. And then there was the viva – the viva voce – the defence of the thesis where Associate Professor Pauline Fatien and Dr Karen Handley put me through my paces. Just look at that list of names I have shared. For anyone in the field, I know you'll agree that that's a pretty awesome bunch of academics.

Now on to the chapter. In this chapter I will share how the research mentioned throughout this book was conducted. This is a summary of the work, and unfortunately I can't include every element – that would be another book in itself. However, my aim is to provide some background for those either interested in understanding more about the literature review and the methodology of the study, or for those interested in pursuing similar

DOI: 10.4324/9781003502494-11

types of qualitative research. The 'findings' from the research as well as the themes from the 'discussion chapter' in the original thesis have been included throughout this book. I therefore won't be covering these in this section of the book but sharing only a brief synopsis. For anyone wanting to read the full thesis, it can be located at the British Library in London, U.K., or at Oxford Brookes University, U.K.

The study was part of a professional doctorate, a doctorate in coaching and mentoring (DCM henceforth) undertaken at Oxford Brookes University between 2019 and 2022. The DCM was an appealing avenue, as it differs from a PhD. In the DCM, participants are part of a small cohort (there were eight of us), and the first part of the programme provides the student with structured modules on qualitative and quantitative research methodologies at doctoral level and the transition to a doctoral level of research. This appealed to me: even though I had successfully completed my masters, also in coaching and mentoring, I considered myself a novice researcher.

Motivation for conducting the research

The research focused on how executive coaches made sense of and enacted duty of care in their roles. I work as an executive coach with corporate organisations, both in the United Kingdom and globally, and have been in the field of learning and development for over thirty years, with the last fifteen being focused on coaching. In my role I have come to understand the complexities involved with multiple parties in coaching relationships. It is common for the executive coach to be working in a triangular relationship including themselves as the coach, the client (the person they are coaching), and the customer (the sponsoring organisation of the person being coached). As a coach, I believe there is a duty of care to the person being coached (the client) and to their organisation (the customer). As a qualified coach supervisor, I believe that my duty of care extends beyond the coach being supervised to the coach's clients.

During the last fifteen years we have seen enormous change in the coaching world. The number of coaches is growing, and I know of coaches who consider themselves qualified after very little training. I have questioned what coaches consider their duty of care and whether they understand the importance of the legalities and of their ethical responsibility. Some coaches strive to fulfil professional body accreditation requirements which are predominantly focused on skill and competence, without stopping to question what that means to them as a coach. I also know of highly experienced coaches who have become disillusioned with the work of the professional coaching bodies to the extent that they are electing not to renew their membership.

The growth of coaching has been exponential and is set to continue. As coaches, I believe we have a responsibility to educate ourselves and to help others, and as this research attests, duty of care is not really talked about. Indeed, an oft-repeated comment by participants who took part in the study was 'this is the first time I've thought about it', the 'it' being duty of care. That is not to say coaches do not think about ethical practice; rather, it is an indication that the concept of duty of care is not clearly or explicitly articulated.

This research provided an opportunity to pause and reflect on how coaches make sense of duty of care and how they enact it. The experience of conducting the study impacted my own coaching practice, and as I delved deeper into the subject, changes were made in how we operate as a business. The sense of duty to the participants who took part in the study has remained throughout, and the thesis aimed to represent their stories and experiences to the best of my abilities as a researcher, both in my thesis and in this book. Most of what follows has been adapted from the thesis, starting with the research aims and objectives.

Research aims and objectives

The aim of the study was to examine how executive coaches make sense of duty of care and how they enact it. The objectives were:

1. To critically review duty of care literature in relation to ethical practice in professional contexts, specifically executive coaching.
2. To explore executive coaches' sensemaking of duty of care and their perceptions of their enactments of duty of care in relation to their own roles, their clients, and coaching.
3. To define duty of care in the context of executive coaching.
4. To contribute to the theory of duty of care and to the development of understanding in how executive coaches develop their professional sense of duty of care and how they enact it.

Brief overview of the research design

The research aim supported the adoption of an inductive approach using participant interviews which enabled the exploration of how the participants made sense of duty of care and their perceptions of how they enacted it. The approach was inductive (Creswell, 2007; Lincoln, Lynham and Guba, 2011; Bryman, 2016), and it was anticipated that coaches' experiences would be situational, subjective, unique, and socially constructed. This approach offered theoretical freedom and flexibility to generate rich and detailed accounts (Braun and Clarke, 2006; Braun, Clarke and Weate, 2017).

Participants were executive coaches with diverse experience, professional training, and coaching body affiliation. Thirty participants were interviewed, and this number was considered appropriate to maximise the opportunity of developing concepts and themes from the data through the broadness of participant perspectives (Baker and Edwards, 2012; Corbin and Strauss, 2015). Participants were recruited through coaching bodies, LinkedIn, and executive coaching supervision groups. I conducted semi-structured interviews lasting approximately sixty minutes, exploring what duty of care meant, how the participants made sense of it, defined it, and enacted it. Data collection and thematic analysis were conducted, with permission from the participants for me to contact them with any clarifying questions following the interviews.

The rest of the chapter will be structured as follows: First, I provide an exploration into the literature review, detailed key areas researched, and gaps identified. This is followed by a walk through the methodology and a discussion on the ontological and epistemological stance taken. The approach used for data collection is explained, and attention is drawn to how rigour and quality of the data collection and analysis were achieved. The chapter ends with a synopsis of the key findings. The previous chapters of the book expand the implications of the findings. The chapters preceding this last section of the book bring the discussion and implications for practitioners to life.

Literature review

The literature review focused on six areas:

1. coaching and duty of care;
2. executive coaching and duty of care;
3. coaching bodies and codes of practice;
4. ethical practice in coaching;
5. duty of care in related professional contexts; and
6. coaches' sensemaking and enactments of duty of care.

As the study was concerned with executive coaching, this area had a predominant role in the literature review. Indeed, coaching has drawn much from related 'helping' professions, and counselling and psychotherapy were selected as two additional fields from which literature was drawn. In addition, sport was included, as the development of sports coaching in relation to duty of care has seen much change in recent years, and the review of the literature gives an insight into what can be learned. It was important to include 'sensemaking' and 'enactment', as these both informed the research paradigm and method adopted, and how the analysis was conducted.

Search terms used included 'executive coaching', 'ethics in coaching', 'coach development in ethics', 'coaching ethics', 'sport ethics', 'care in sport', 'helping professions', 'ethics in helping professions', 'duty of care', 'making sense', 'sensemaking', and 'enactment'. Literature was sourced from peer-reviewed journals in relevant fields through search engines including Google Scholar (from where I would take the results and use Brookes Library to source the articles), PsychINFO, ProQuest, Research-Gate, and Brookes' RADAR repository for e-theses and dissertations. Literature was also sourced from academic and practitioner textbooks on coaching and the related fields of sports coaching and 'helping' professions. A further source of literature was from the coaching bodies, in the form of their ethical codes of practice, a conversation with the Global Chair of the ICF Ethics Independent Review Board (IRB, 2021), and a report shared from them.

I decided that gaining understanding of literature that discussed development in coaching more broadly would also be helpful, as reviewing literature on duty of care in isolation would not inform how this research topic related to coaching literature generally. Therefore, systematic literature reviews and meta-analyses of literature reviews about coaching were examined (De Meuse, Dai and Lee, 2009; Ely, Boyce, Nelson, Zaccaro, Hernez-Broome and Whyman, 2010; Lai and McDowall, 2014; Theeboom, Beersma and Van Vianen, 2014; Sonesh, Coultas, Lacerenza, Marlow, Benishek and Salas, 2015; Blackman, Moscardo and Gray, 2016; Burt and Talati, 2017; Athanasopoulou and Dopson, 2018; Bozer and Jones, 2018; de Haan, 2019; Schermuly and Graßmann, 2019; Graßmann, Schölmerich and Schermuly, 2020; Müller and Kotte, 2020; Pandolfi, 2020), a brief overview of which follows.

The 15 systematic and meta-analysis literature reviews in coaching and executive coaching from 2009 to 2020 were examined chronologically, a timeline which I'll now share briefly. De Meuse et al. (2009) researched the return on investment of executive coaching. Six observations made by them included how coaching works and the impact of coaching. The sustained theme in coaching literature on outcomes and evaluation of effectiveness ensued with the presentation of an integrated framework of coaching evaluation of clients' leadership behaviours (Ely et al., 2010). Theeboom et al. (2014) further contribute to the dialogue by questioning whether coaching has an effect on categories of performance and skills, wellbeing, coping, work attitudes, and goal-directed self-regulation.

The focus then turns slightly, as Lai and McDowall (2014) focus on the effective attributes of the coaching psychologist, and five key factors are identified for enhancing the coaching process, including trust, managing coachees' difficulties, two-way communication, clear contracting, and a transparent process. A gap of two years sees the return to the topic of coaching variables in how coaching effectiveness is conceptualised (Sonesh et al., 2015) and, once again, a review on the exploration of effectiveness in workplace coaching (Blackman et al., 2016). The interest in the topic of investigating outcomes and the value of executive coaching comes to the fore once more in Burt and Talati (2017), followed by Bozer and Jones (2018), who investigated factors that determine workplace coaching effectiveness.

In 2018, the field's obsessive focus on the end or destination and outcomes of coaching, specifically executive coaching, is criticised (Athanasopoulou and Dopson, 2018). The following year provides some practical suggestions on how coaching can benefit from training and supervision, amongst other points (de Haan, 2019). Schermuly and Graßmann (2019) change the narrative by turning attention to the negative effects of coaching. Theirs is the first systematic or meta-analysis to draw attention to coaches fulfilling their ethical requirements. Their research highlights the benefit of supervision in mitigating negative effects in coaching and the importance of a higher quality of relationship between the coach and the client. The three remaining systematic meta-analysis studies turn attention once more to the relationship between working alliance and coaching outcomes, goal activities with coaching outcomes, and coach characteristics (Graßmann et al., 2020; Müller and Kotte, 2020; Pandolfi, 2020).

With the exception of Athanasopoulou and Dopson (2018) and Schermuly and Graßmann (2019), minimal attention is drawn to contracting and matters of ethics in coaching. A conversation across the systematic and meta-analysis literature reviews specifically on ethics and coaching is lacking.

Once the systematic and meta-analysis reviews were completed, attention was given to the following six areas: literature relating to coaching and duty of care, executive coaching and duty of care, coaching bodies and codes of practice, ethical practice in coaching, duty of care in related professional contexts, and coaches' sensemaking and enactments of duty of care. Again, this chapter provides a very reduced snapshot of all of this.

Table 10.1 provides a brief overview of what I have shared. Under each section, a description of what was reviewed is shown, with an example research source, followed by an overview of the main gaps identified.

The literature review demonstrates how duty of care in coaching is an underdeveloped research area. In addition to the systematic and

Table 10.1 Overview of Literature Review

Literature reviewed on systematic coaching literature reviews and meta-analysis coaching literature reviews conducted between 2009 and 2022 (De Meuse et al., 2009; Ely et al., 2010; Lai and McDowall, 2014; Theeboom et al., 2014; Sonesh et al., 2015; Blackman et al., 2016; Burt and Talati, 2017; Athanasopoulou and Dopson, 2018; Bozer and Jones, 2018; de Haan, 2019; Schermuly and Graßmann, 2019; Graßmann et al., 2020; Müller and Kotte, 2020; Pandolfi, 2020).

Literature Relating to Coaching and Duty of Care	Literature Relating to Executive Coaching and Duty of Care	Literature Relating to Coaching Bodies and Codes of Practice	Literature Relating to Ethical Practice in Coaching	Literature Relating to Duty of Care in Related Professional Contexts	Literature Relating to Coaches' Sensemaking and Enactments of Duty of Care
How duty of care is defined in the context of coaching. Literature on coaching and the law. The use of ethical codes of practice by coaches. Professional coaching bodies and their role in duty of care for coaches. Ethical practice in coaching (e.g., Lindberg and Desmond, 2006; Williams, 2006; Iordanou, Hawley and Iordanou, 2017; Wright and O'Connor, 2021).	Literature on the role of the executive coach. How the executive coach develops in relation to duty of care. Ethical conflicts experienced by executive coaches and how they deal with them. Relationship management for the executive coach within their complex multi-stakeholder engagements (e.g., Spence, Cavanagh and Grant, 2006; Athanasopoulou and Dopson, 2018).	Literature on best practice for coaches. Codes of conduct and ethical practice for coaches who are members of coaching bodies (e.g., ICF, EMCC, APECS, AC; Diochon and Nizet, 2015, 2019).	Contemporary theoretical sources which have helped shape understanding of ethical best practice (e.g., Iordanou et al., 2017; Brennan and Wildflower, 2018; Diochon and Nizet, 2015, 2019).	Duty of care in related professional contexts of counselling and psychotherapy. Duty of care in sports coaching. A sports coach's responsibility to care. Regulatory practice in 'helping' professions. Practitioner developments in relation to duty of care (e.g., Mitchels and Bond, 2010; Bond, 2015; Cronin and Armour, 2017, 2019; Partington, 2017, 2021).	Making sense of sensemaking and the meaning of enactment in their broadest terms. Understanding sensemaking and enactment in organisational and individual contexts. Making sense and enactment in relation to ethical matters for the coach (e.g., Weick, 1995; Diochon and Nizet, 2019; Pichault, Diochon and Nizet, 2020).

Overview of main gaps identified

○ Limited attention to how executive coaches make sense of ethical dilemmas, except for one study, which specifically relates to using codes of ethics (Diochon and Nizet, 2015, 2019).

○ Limited attention with empirical evidence on how executive coaches make sense of ethical dilemmas in coaching.

○ No empirical data on executive coaches' perceptions of their enactments of duty of care.

○ The role of the executive coach is defined by multiple authors, and literature is present on the role; no gap in this part of the literature reviewed (e.g., Peltier, 2010).

○ Duty of care in coaching literature is not clearly defined, unlike in related professional contexts.

○ Ethics research most closely related to duty of care in coaching is narrow and concerned with coaches who are members of coaching bodies, and their use of ethical codes of practice; only one study of coach interpretation and execution of codes of ethics when facing an ethical dilemma. There is no research which includes coaches who are not members of coaching bodies (Diochon and Nizet, 2015, 2019).

○ Limited literature is available on coaching and the law, unlike in related professional contexts.

○ Ethical codes of practice in coaching are mainly focused on competency and skills, not explicitly on ethical and moral duty.

○ One study on duty of care in coaching, 'an unregulated profession' (Spence et al., 2006).

○ Main literature on ethical practice in coaching is found in textbooks, with paucity of primary research (e.g., Iordanou et al., 2017; Brennan and Wildflower, 2018).

meta-analysis reviews, six areas of literature were included in the literature review, as presented in Table 10.1: literature relating to coaching and duty of care, executive coaching and duty of care, coaching bodies and codes of practice, ethical practice in coaching, duty of care in related professional contexts, and coaches' sensemaking and enactments of duty of care.

Literature relating to duty of care in coaching is sparse, with only minimal texts available on coaching and the law (Lindberg and Desmond, 2006; Williams, 2006; Wright and O'Connor, 2021). Even though the number of coaches has increased in recent years, the conversation in the literature on a coach's duty of care has not. A duty of care applies to a coach's legal responsibilities and to their ethical and moral practice (Williams, 2006; Iordanou et al., 2017), yet research is lacking on what this means to coaches and how they enact it.

Literature more specifically related to executive coaching highlights how executive coaches are not held to particular professional standards (Peltier, 2010) but are autonomous in an unregulated environment (Spence et al., 2006). Their roles are complex due to multiple stakeholders in the coaching relationship (Athanasopoulou and Dopson, 2018), typically their client, their customer, and themselves. Yet how their duty of care relates to their interactions with those involved in a coaching relationship, and the wider system, is not known.

Ethical codes go some way towards providing coaches with frameworks for how to manage conflicts of interest, conduct, integrity, contracting, and other matters, yet the literature criticises coaching bodies for moving towards competence and skill bases (Bachkirova, 2017). Furthermore, duty of care does not feature explicitly in ethical codes (GCE, ICF Code of Ethics). Complaints raised to coaching bodies are increasing (IRB, 2021) and the literature argues for education in ethics for coaches to be placed centrally in coaches' development (Diochon and Nizet, 2015). Codes of conduct and best practice signpost professional best practice, yet the literature does not provide sufficiently explored domains and boundaries of duty of care for executive coaches. What is evident from the coaching bodies is an inherent responsibility for the coach to act in good faith, serving the needs of the client (ICF, EMCC, AC), and to operate within the laws of the country within which they practice (Wright and O'Connor, 2021). However, research is lacking on coaches' experiences in this regard.

Primary research on coaches' perspectives on matters relating to ethical practice and duty of care in coaching is also lacking, with literature sources mainly focusing on ethical best practice (Peltier, 2010; Iordanou et al., 2017; Brennan and Wildflower, 2018). Coaches are unlikely to refer to an ethical code at times when ethical conflicts arise but instead revert to dialogue with supervisors or peers.

There is a greater understanding of duty of care in related professional contexts, such as in nursing. In sport, the distinction between ethical and unethical behaviour is less clear, with sports coaches being responsible for the climate of the coaching (Loughead, Patterson and Carron, 2008; Burton, Peachey and Wells, 2017; Lyle, 2019). Education and training of sports coaches in matters relating to duty of care feature in the literature as a required addition, with dialogue now turning to its importance (Partington, 2017, 2021), yet this aspect is currently lacking in coaching literature.

Research on ethics of the coach most closely related to duty of care is narrow and focuses on coaches who have affiliation to a coaching body and their use of codes of practice. Only one primary research study is present in coaching literature evidencing how coaches make sense of ethical dilemmas (Diochon and Nizet, 2019), which further demonstrates the complex nature of the executive coach's role (Pichault et al., 2020). Yet this study included only participants who were members of a coaching body, and it focused on sensemaking during ethical dilemmas. Including the voices of coaches who are not members of a coaching body and exploring their sensemaking of duty of care more broadly and how they enact it – and not only during ethical dilemmas – would be a valuable contribution to the literature.

Methodology

A qualitative, inductive approach was adopted, using interview research and working reflexively with thematic analysis to enable the exploration of how the participants made sense of duty of care, and their perceptions of how they enacted it (Creswell, 2007; Bryman, 2016; Braun et al., 2017; Braun and Clarke, 2006, 2022). One-on-one qualitative interviewing is a commonly used method in qualitative research (Bryman and Bell, 2015; Mason, 2018), and was selected as the appropriate approach for this research project. The interview is a conversation between researcher and participant, where the researcher's aim is to obtain desired information in line with the objectives. As the researcher, I operated from the perspective that knowledge is situated and contextual (Mason, 2018), with the interview acting as a construction of that knowledge.

Open-ended questions were used, fitting a constructivist paradigm (Lincoln et al., 2011), an approach which also positions the researcher within the context of the research. As the researcher, I brought my own experience into the exploration of the data and engaged with the participants through dialogue, with constructivism being used to reconstruct understandings of the participants' worlds (Denzin and Lincoln, 2011). I decided to use qualitative interviewing, as a constructivist ontological position supports the suggestion that participants' knowledge, understanding, interpretation, experiences, perceptions, and sensemaking are meaningful properties of their social reality (Mason, 2018), and this supported the research questions being explored.

In today's postmodern society, interviews are common, with participants most often familiar with the activity of taking part in an interview (Aarsand and Aarsand, 2019). As the researcher, I was interested in the participants' points of view (Bryman and Bell, 2015) and asking questions in a semi-structured interview format would meet the research aim. Participants would have freedom and flexibility in how they replied (Bryman and Bell, 2015), which also fitted ontologically. Once the interviews had been conducted, inductive thematic analysis followed.

As the research aim warranted a constructivist approach, I considered using thematic analysis where the data would be analysed to find themes that related to the aim rather than approaching the analysis from a theoretical stance. Indeed, analysing from a theoretical approach provides the researcher with a more detailed analysis of some aspects of the data, being theory led from existent knowledge, rather than allowing the research question to evolve through the coding process (Braun and Clarke, 2006, 2022). Yet an inductive approach follows the assumption that the themes identified are strongly linked to the data and the final output might have little resemblance to the questions asked. In support of this methodological approach, I would code the data without trying to fit it into any pre-existent code framework nor any of my own theories, retaining the flexibility and reflexivity that thematic analysis permits (Braun and Clarke, 2022).

However, there was tension here between my goal as the researcher to answer the research question, and allowing the data to lead the theme generation. At some points, I experienced a sense of moving quite a distance away from the questions that were answered in the interviews, when themes identified had no resemblance to the interview questions. This was counterbalanced by keeping the research aim centrally in focus, acknowledging that not all data would be relevant nor included. The strong sense of duty to the participants' accounts yet also to the research aim remained. I experienced an internal battle at times on how to be dutiful to both, and I describe it as a sense of needing to be courageous in trusting the methodological approach taken, and trusting that the research aim would be achieved with ontological and epistemological congruence.

I did not have a pre-determined theory on what duty of care meant and consciously approached the research from an inductive position, keeping the interview questions broad and general so the participants had the opportunity to construct meaning (Creswell, 2007). The aim was to have theoretical freedom and flexibility so that rich and detailed accounts in alignment with a constructivist research paradigm could be generated by thematic analysis (Braun and Clarke, 2006, 2022) whilst demonstrating trustworthiness in the research (Yardley, 2008; Tracy, 2010; Lincoln et al., 2011).

Exploring ontology and epistemology

The research was concerned with exploring and understanding how executive coaches made sense of duty of care and how they enacted it. Ontology is concerned with the nature of reality; epistemology with our knowledge of it (Silverman, 2020). Whilst considering the ontological position for this research and the nature of reality, I deliberated on my own world view as well as the commitments needed to deliver the research aim. As an executive coach I work with people, their experience, and their reflections. Each situation is unique and specific to the client involved, often complex, with multiple actors involved in the executive coaches' topics brought to sessions. Meaning is constructed by the client through reflection and dialogue exchange. As the coach, whilst not directive, I am involved in that dialogue exchange and am consequently engaged in the co-creation of the thinking that occurs. I hold the view that our realities are created from our interactions, with our perceptions socially constructed, ever changing and relative to the situation we are in.

Considering the commitments needed to deliver the research aim, I anticipated coaches' experiences would be situational, subjective, unique, and socially constructed, with meaning being arrived at through their interactions (Lincoln et al., 2011). Similarly, coaching is an interaction between two people. In both scenarios of the research and in coaching, our individual experience of a dialogue exchange (be it coach/client or research/participant) would be different, and what we consider real would be in our minds (Creswell, 2007). Ontologically, reality in these two scenarios is constructed in the minds of those involved through each experience (Lincoln et al., 2011); it is relative to the individual – it lies in our minds as the actors involved.

I understand the inherent challenges of working as a coach and appreciate that it is not a prescriptive role – there is not only one single approach. Executive coaches operate independently, and each assignment is unique. Understanding this, the constructivist stance in the research was underpinned by the assumption that there would be complexity with multiple meanings. Within constructivist research paradigms, the focus is on the diversity and multiplicity of meanings, which leads researchers to explore a wide range of perspectives rather than condensing them into a few specific categories (Creswell, 2007).

I anticipated that meanings from the participants would be subjective and negotiated socially by each of them. Furthermore, I was not seeking to categorise narrowly but wanted theoretical freedom to work with the data (Braun and Clarke, 2006, 2022) without the restrictions of rules and principles of positivist paradigms (Boyatzis, 1998). Instead, I worked flexibly, making decisions through the inquiry on what counted as observations, what design would be acceptable to meet the needs of the research aim, and what problems would be worthy of attention (Mir and Watson, 2000).

Although similarities between being a coach and a researcher were evident, it was challenging to adopt a purist ontological stance. Part of the research aim for the study was to explore how the participants made sense of duty of care. Weick (1995) argues that sensemaking can be a retrospective fit as we freeze moments of a given time, and the researcher can fall into 'ontological oscillation', a common hazard for researchers (Weick, 1995). Yet this ontological oscillation is common in everyday life as people make sense of experiences, with no care about ontology.

The researcher who is researching how people make sense of others' experiences must therefore also oscillate (Colville and Pye, 2010). Experiences and perceptions are inseparable from the world and consciousness, and an objective world does not exist independently from our perceptions of it (Mason, 2018), so oscillation is inevitable. Weick (1995) argues that ontological oscillation is prevalent in all forms of phenomenological research, unavoidably, as the researcher attempts to operationalise their ideas. Given that individuals navigate multiple identities and realities, it is unreasonable to expect them to strictly adhere to one ontological perspective – such a demand would restrict their ability to make sense of the world (Weick, 1995). When the researcher freezes a moment of narrative in an interview, they are moving to a more realist ontology.

In my quest for clarity on the research paradigm, I found myself moving to a point of acceptance that oscillation would inevitably occur, but that the pendulum swing would move back to a constructivist ontology. Perhaps it was unsurprising that this part of the thinking was challenging and multivalent, as I uncovered definitions, methods, and practices which traversed multiple disciplines in the qualitative research field, since qualitative research is many things to many people (Denzin and Lincoln, 2011).

Regarding my epistemological position, as the researcher, I recognised how my own culture, background and life experiences would shape the interpretation of the interviews as I was also positioned in the research.

Adopting a constructivist epistemology assumes that we cannot separate ourselves from what we know; we each understand the world through our own frame of reference (Lincoln et al., 2011). Indeed, the research and I would be linked.

Data collection and analysis

The research involved introduction calls with potential participants followed by sixty-minute semi-structured interviews. The aim of the interviews was to explore how the participants made sense of duty of care and their perceptions of how they enacted it. I considered that approximately thirty participants would be appropriate, thus maximising the opportunity of developing concepts and themes from the data through the broadness of the participants' perspectives (Corbin and Strauss, 2015; Baker and Edwards, 2012).

Figure 10.1 shows the steps taken in the research instrument design, data collection, and data analysis.

The research design involved developing the interview framework, testing it as a pilot, and adapting and modifying it following the pilot interviews before deciding on the final interview structure. Participants took part in an introduction call, a valuable part of the research process which helped build rapport and enabled assessment of the eligibility of the participants. Once the interviews were completed, the arduous task of transcribing and data cleaning (including anonymising and redacting) commenced. The transcripts amounted to 1,300 pages of A4 text, and detailed scrutiny was given to each and every page. This was an important part, as it enabled me to get close to the data. Coding involved several stages, and a detailed explanation of this process can be found in the original thesis. In summary, there were four rounds of coding before a hierarchical evaluation of categories led to theme generation. The theme generation was refined and developed into the final super-ordinate and sub-ordinate themes, leading to the findings.

Rigour and quality

Tracy's (2010) conceptualisation of criteria for achieving quality in qualitative research was used as the guide to question and ensure trustworthiness in this study. The eight criteria were adopted as a tool and this was used alongside the research process. Table 10.2 presents Tracy's (2010) eight criteria, with commentary and reflections on how each was achieved in relation to my research.

Honouring the commitments to the research, to the participants and to myself as the researcher was core to the study. In addition to using Tracy's

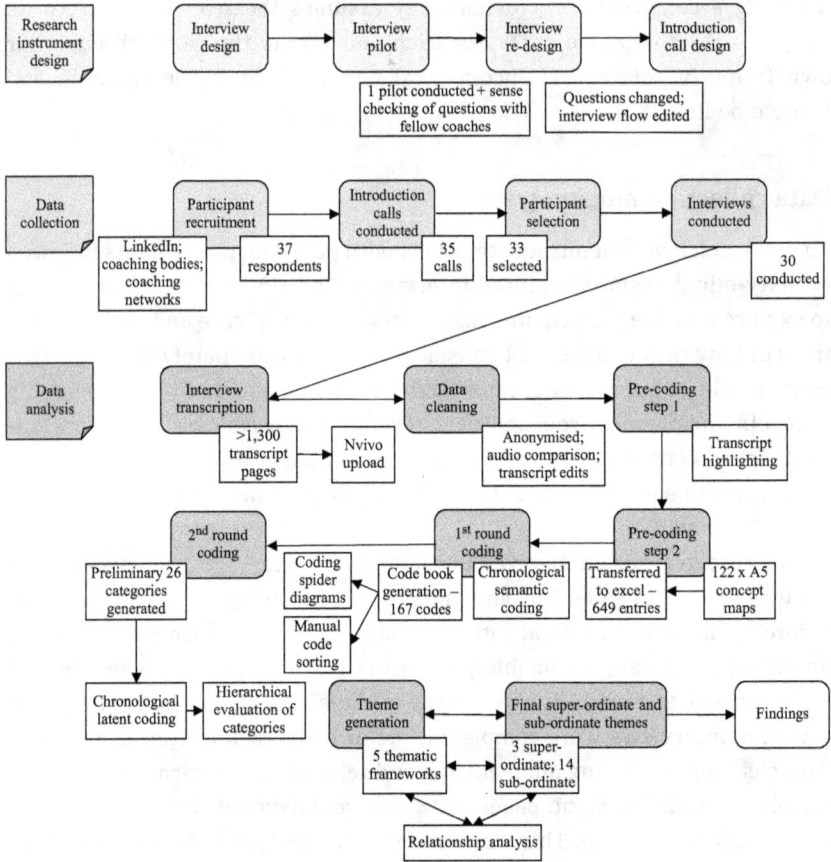

Figure 10.1 Data collection and analysis

(2010) criteria as discussed, I used five key questions throughout as a reminder for questioning the ethical and legal considerations (Mason, 2018, p. 102), and my own duty of care to the participants:

1. Have I honoured my commitment about confidentiality and privacy?
2. Have I acted in the spirit of the informed consent which I received?
3. Have I fulfilled my aims with epistemological ethics to produce good-quality, valid research?
4. Have I used my research, and my explanations, effectively and ethically?
5. Have I generalised appropriately?

Table 10.2 Rigour and Quality Using Tracy's (2010) Criteria

Tracy (2010) Criteria for Quality	Means, Practices, Methods (Tracy, 2010)	Researcher Reflections on How the Criteria Were Met (Mayhead, 2022)
Worthy topic	The topic of the research is relevant, timely, significant, interesting.	The topic of duty of care in coaching has not been researched, nor is duty of care in coaching clearly defined. As duty of care sits within the ethical framework of a coach's practice, it was considered important for coach development and coach practice for this area to be researched. At a time when the number of coaches is continually growing, this study is relevant and significant to coaching.
Rich rigour	The study uses sufficient, abundant, appropriate, and complex theoretical constructs, data and time in the field, sample, context, data collection, and analysis processes.	Thirty executive coaches were interviewed, thus providing a broad spectrum of experiences and perspectives, aimed at demonstrating sufficient data was gathered. Time was spent in the field and in the data analysis, a process that was not expedited, but diligence in thoroughness was demonstrated through the pre-coding stages of analysis and into the coding, all of which is presented in detail.
Sincerity	The study is characterised by self-reflexivity about the researcher's subjective values, biases and inclinations, and transparency about the methods and challenges.	Self-reflexivity was practised throughout the research process and at times I was aware that my own continual questioning of actions and decisions was leading to self-doubt. Being humble and vulnerable is needed, and I have aimed to be transparent about the research process in great detail.
Credibility	The research is marked by thick description, concrete detail, explication of tacit (nontextual) knowledge, showing rather than telling, triangulation or crystallisation, multivocality, and member reflections.	I immersed myself in the interview transcripts for many weeks, thus developing a tacit knowledge of what was shared. The findings are presented with bountiful relevant quotes from the participants to present thick description for the reader. The voices of the participants and researchers in the field and also my own voice have been included.

(Continued)

Table 10.2 (Continued)

Tracy (2010) Criteria for Quality	Means, Practices, Methods (Tracy, 2010)	Researcher Reflections on How the Criteria Were Met (Mayhead, 2022)
Resonance	The research influences, affects, or moves particular readers or a variety of audiences through aesthetic, evocative representation, naturalistic generalisations, transferable findings.	In conducting this research it was important to ensure the work has relevance to coaches, with coaches being able to apply the research to their own actions and situations. Practical implications for coaching relevant to coaches, coach supervisors, coaching bodies, coach training providers, and buyers of coaching have been discussed.
Significant contribution	The research provides a significant contribution conceptually/theoretically, practically, morally, methodologically, heuristically.	This research contributes to theoretical knowledge, and to practice. Duty of care of the coach has not previously been researched and this study situates the subject in coaching literature. A definition of duty of care for the coach has been developed. This is the first study to find 'care' being central to the role of the coach.
Ethical	The research considers procedural ethics, situational and culturally specific ethics, relational ethics, exiting ethics.	My university, Oxford Brookes, has strict research protocols which were followed ardently and enabled procedural ethics to be honoured. Each interview was different, which required adoption of situational ethical awareness and reflection on my own decisions, which were journaled. I adopted a relational ethic of care through having respect for the participants and creating connectedness, giving thanks and appreciation. Whilst I cannot control how my work will be read, I have endeavoured to portray the research in its truest form, respecting the accounts and experiences shared by the participants.
Meaningful coherence	The study achieves what it purports to be about, uses methods and procedures that fit its stated goals, and meaningfully interconnects the literature, research questions, findings, and interpretations with each other.	The research aim and objectives have been met, and the research was conducted with ontological congruence in not looking for one single truth but through exploring multiple perspectives of the participants. The findings attend to the research question and the reviewed literature situates the findings.

Brief overview of findings

As mentioned at the start of this chapter, this whole book is an exploration of the 'findings' and the 'discussion' from the thesis. But to summarise them briefly, the findings showed that coaches made sense of duty of care through drawing primarily from their own life experiences and role models, and their own development as coaches – their sensemaking was formed less from coaching bodies, ethical codes, and the law. Their own life experiences and coach development informed their understanding of duty of care and their perceptions of how they enacted it.

The findings also showed how coaches had developed a duty *to* care, a duty of needing to care both for their clients and for themselves. They perceived contracting as being central in the coaching relationship and how they enacted their duty of care, and this included endings and how they put their own oxygen mask on first. Caring was also hazardous for some participants as coaches, and it led to over-caring. This had an impact on coaches, creating a sense of a lasting duty which sometimes remained indefinitely. Coaches talked of the emotional burden they sometimes experienced, especially when ending coaching engagements. The coach is central to the coaching relationship, and the findings show how the coaches considered that, as practitioners, they had a duty of care to themselves, through self-care. Finally, the findings show how the coach's reach of duty of care is systemic, going beyond the coach and client relationship, and to the customer. Furthermore, some coaches considered they had a duty of care beyond the customer and to extremities of the client's interactions outside of the coaching relationship, often unseen by the coach.

Concluding thoughts

The aim of this chapter is to share insights into the method used behind the research study, not to debate and discuss the findings. The previous chapters provide that opportunity. To fellow researchers curious to understand more, I hope insight into the study provides inspiration and also trust in the rigour adopted around the methodology. The chapter provides the opportunity for the reader to explore more around the literature review, the meta-analyses and systematic reviews that informed the basis of the study.

Whilst it isn't possible to include every detail, I hope this chapter has provided you with some additional thinking, perhaps a greater curiosity about the literature, or an interest in research methodology, rigour, and robustness and has demystified some of what goes on in the solitude of research.

References

Aarsand, L. and Aarsand, P. (2019) 'Framing and switches at the outset of qualitative research interviews', *Qualitative Research*, 19(6), pp. 635–652. https://doi.org/10.1177/1468794118816623

Athanasopoulou, A. and Dopson, S. (2018) 'A systematic review of executive coaching outcomes: Is it the journey or the destination that matters the most?', *The Leadership Quarterly*, 29(1), pp. 70–88. https://doi.org/10.1016/j.leaqua.2017.11.004

Bachkirova, T. (2017) 'Developing a knowledge base of coaching: Questions to explore'. https://radar.brookes.ac.uk/radar/items/f15792ac-730f-45f2-b087-22b819be6239/1/   https://doi.org/10.1037/0003-066X.46.4.422

Baker, S. and Edwards, R. (2012) 'How many qualitative interviews is enough?' *National Centre for Research Centre Review Papers*. https://eprints.ncrm.ac.uk/id/eprint/2273/4/how_many_interviews.pdf

Blackman, A., Moscardo, G. and Gray, D. (2016) 'Challenges for the theory and practice of business coaching: A systematic review of empirical evidence', *Human Resource Development Review*, 15(4), pp. 459–486.

Bond, T. (2015) *Standards and ethics for counselling in action*. 4th Ed. London: Sage. p. 306. *Book*. 2nd Ed. Thousand Oaks, CA: Sage.

Boyatzis, R.E. (1998) *Transforming qualitative information: Thematic analysis and code development*. Thousand Oaks, CA: Sage Publications.

Bozer, G. and Jones, R.J. (2018) 'Understanding the factors that determine workplace coaching effectiveness: A systematic literature review', *European Journal of Work and Organizational Psychology*, 27(3), pp. 342–361. https://doi.org/10.1080/1359432X.2018.1446946

Braun, V. and Clarke, V. (2006) 'Using thematic analysis in psychology', *Qualitative Research in Psychology*, 3(2), pp. 77–101. https://doi.org/10.1191/1478088706qp063oa

Braun, V. and Clarke, V. (2022) 'Conceptual and design thinking for thematic analysis', *Qualitative Psychology*, 9(1), pp. 3–26. https://doi.org/10.1037/qup0000196

Braun, V., Clarke, V. and Weate, P. (2017) 'Using thematic analysis in sport and exercise research', In *Handbook of qualitative research in sport and exercise*, eds. B. Smith and A.C. Sparkes. London: Routledge Taylor and Francis Group. pp. 191–205.

Brennan, D. and Wildflower, L. (2018) 'Ethics in coaching', In *The complete handbook of coaching*, eds. E. Cox, T. Bachkirova, and D. Clutterbuck. 3rd Ed. London: Sage. pp. 500–517.

Bryman, A. (2016) *Social research methods*. UK: Oxford University Press.

Bryman, A. and Bell, E. (2015) *Business research methods*. Vol. 4. Glasgow: Bell & Bain Ltd.

Burt, D. and Talati, Z. (2017) 'The unsolved value of executive coaching: A meta-analysis of outcomes using randomised control trial studies', *International Journal of Evidence Based Coaching and Mentoring*, 15(2), pp. 17–24. https://doi.org/10.24384/000248

Burton, L., Peachey, J. and Wells, J. (2017) 'The role of servant leadership in developing an ethical climate in sport organizations', *Journal of Sport Management*, 31(3), pp. 229–240. https://doi.org/10.1123/jsm.2016-0047

Colville, I. and Pye, A. (2010) 'A sensemaking perspective on network pictures', *Industrial Marketing Management*, 39(3), pp. 372–380. https://doi.org/10.1016/j.indmarman.2009.03.012

Corbin, J. and Strauss, A. (2015) *Basics of qualitative research: Techniques and procedures for developing grounded theory.* 4th Ed. Thousand Oaks, CA: Sage.

Creswell, J. (2007) *Qualitative inquiry and research design: Choosing among five approaches.* 2nd Ed. Thousand Oaks, CA: Sage.

Cronin, C. and Armour, K. (2017) '"Being" in the coaching world: New insights on youth performance coaching from an interpretative phenomenological approach', *Sport, Education and Society*, 22(8), pp. 919–931. https://doi.org/10.1080/13573322.2015.1108912

Cronin, C. and Armour, K. (eds) (2019) *Care in sport coaching: Pedagogical cases.* Abingdon, Oxon: Routledge (Routledge research in sports coaching). https://doi.org/10.4324/9781351109314

de Haan, E. (2019) 'A systematic review of qualitative studies in workplace and executive coaching: The emergence of a body of research', *Consulting Psychology Journal: Practice and Research*, 71(4), p. 227. https://doi.org/10.1037/cpb0000144

De Meuse, K., Dai, G. and Lee, R. (2009) 'Evaluating the effectiveness of executive coaching: Beyond ROI?', *Coaching: An International Journal of Theory, Research and Practice*, 2(2), pp. 117–134. https://doi.org/10.1080/17521880902882413

Denzin, N. and Lincoln, Y. (2011) *The sage handbook of qualitative research.* 4th Ed. Thousand Oaks, CA: Sage.

Diochon, P.F. and Nizet, J. (2015) 'Ethical codes and executive coaches: One size does not fit all', *The Journal of Applied Behavioral Science*, 51(2), pp. 277–301. https://doi.org/10.1177/0021886315576190

Diochon, P.F. and Nizet, J. (2019) 'Ethics as a fabric: An emotional reflexive sensemaking process', *Business Ethics Quarterly*, 29(4), pp. 461–489. https://doi.org/10.1017/beq.2019.11

Ely, K., Boyce, L., Nelson, J., Zaccaro, S., Hernez-Broome, G. and Whyman, W. (2010) 'Evaluating leadership coaching: A review and integrated framework', *The Leadership Quarterly*, 21(4), pp. 585–599. https://doi.org/10.1016/j.leaqua.2010.06.003

Graßmann, C., Schölmerich, F. and Schermuly, C. (2020) 'The relationship between working alliance and client outcomes in coaching: A meta-analysis', *Human Relations*, 73(1), pp. 35–58. https://doi.org/10.1177/0018726718819725

Iordanou, I., Hawley, R. and Iordanou, C. (2017) *Values and ethics in coaching.* London: Sage. https://doi.org/10.4135/9781473983755

IRB (2021) *International Coach Federation, Annual report, Independent Review Board.* Unpublished.

Lai, Y. and McDowall, A. (2014) 'A systematic review (SR) of coaching psychology: Focusing on the attributes of effective coaching psychologists', *International Coaching Psychology Review,* 9(2), pp. 118–134. https://doi.org/10.53841/bpsicpr.2014.9.2.118

Lincoln, Y., Lynham, S. and Guba, E. (2011) 'Paradigmatic controversies, contradictions, and emerging confluences, revisited', *The Sage Handbook of Qualitative Research*, 4(2), pp. 97–128.

Lindberg, W. and Desmond, A. (2006) *'Legal issues and solutions for coaches', Law and ethics in coaching: How to solve and avoid difficult problems in your practice.* John Wiley & Sons. https://learning.oreilly.com/library/view/law-and-ethics/9780471716143/xhtml/Chapter08.html

Loughead, T., Patterson, M. and Carron, A. (2008) 'The impact of fitness leader behaviours and cohesion on an exerciser's affective state',

International Journal of Sport and Exercise Psychology, 6(1), pp. 53–68. https://doi.org/10.1080/1612197X.2008.9671854

Lyle, J. (2019) 'What is ethical coaching?', *International Journal of Coaching Science*, 13(1).

Mason, J. (2018) *Qualitative researching*. London: Sage.

Mayhead, B. (2022) 'Duty of care in coaching: From ethical frameworks to the development of the coach', Doctoral thesis. Oxford Brookes University. https://doi.org/10.24384/sjmq-9b67

Mir, R. and Watson, A. (2000) 'Strategic management and the philosophy of science: The case for a constructivist methodology', *Strategic Management Journal*, 21(9), pp. 941–953.

Mitchels, B. and Bond, T. (2010) *Essential law for counsellors and psychotherapists*. London: Sage.

Müller, A. and Kotte, S. (2020) 'Of SMART, GROW and goals gone wild: A systematic literature review on the relevance of goal activities in workplace coaching', *International Coaching Psychology Review*, 15(2), pp. 69–97.

Pandolfi, C. (2020) 'Active ingredients in executive coaching: A systematic literature review', *International Coaching Psychology Review*, 15(2), pp. 6–30. https://doi.org/10.53841/bpsicpr.2020.15.2.6

Partington, N. (2017) 'Sports coaching and the law of negligence: Implications for coaching practice', *Sports Coaching Review*, 6(1), pp. 36–56. https://doi.org/10.1080/21640629.2016.1180860

Partington, N. (2021) *Coaching, sport and the law: A duty of care*. New York: Routledge Taylor and Francis Group. https://doi.org/10.4324/9780429343148

Peltier, B. (2010) *The psychology of executive coaching: Theory and application*. 2nd Ed. New York: Routledge Taylor and Francis Group. https://doi.org/10.4324/9780203886106

Pichault, F., Diochon, P.F. and Nizet, J. (2020) 'Autonomy of independent professionals: A political process perspective', *European Management Journal*, 38(4), pp. 623–633. https://doi.org/10.1016/j.emj.2019.12.007

Schermuly, C. and Graßmann, C. (2019) 'A literature review on negative effects of coaching – What we know and what we need to know', *Coaching: An International Journal of Theory, Research and Practice,* 12(1), pp. 39–66. https://doi.org/10.1080/17521882.2018.1528621

Silverman, D. (2020) *Interpreting qualitative data*. London: Sage.

Sonesh, S., Coultas, C., Lacerenza, C., Marlow, S., Benishek, L. and Salas, E. (2015) 'The power of coaching: A meta-analytic investigation', *Coaching: An International Journal of Theory, Research and Practice*, 8(2), pp. 73–95. https://doi.org/10.1080/17521882.2015.1071418

Spence, G., Cavanagh, M. and Grant, A. (2006) 'Duty of care in an unregulated industry: Initial findings on the diversity and practices of Australian coaches', *International Coaching Psychology Review*, 1(1), pp. 71–85.

Theeboom, T., Beersma, B. and Van Vianen, A. (2014) 'Does coaching work? A meta-analysis on the effects of coaching on individual level outcomes in an organizational context', *The Journal of Positive Psychology*, 9(1), pp. 1–18. https://doi.org/10.1080/17439760.2013.837499

Tracy, S. (2010) 'Qualitative quality: Eight "big-tent" criteria for excellent qualitative research', *Qualitative Inquiry*, 16(10), pp. 837–851. https://doi.org/10.1177/1077800410383121

Weick, K. (1995) *Sensemaking in organizations*. Sage.

Williams, P. (2006) 'The profession of coaching. Law and ethics in coaching – how to solve and avoid difficult problems', In *Your practice*. Hoboken, NJ: John Wiley and Sons. pp. 3–20.

Wright, A. and O'Connor, S. (2021) 'Supervision for working legally', In *Coaching and mentoring supervision: Theory and practice.* 2nd Ed. UK: McGraw-Hill Education.

Yardley, L. (2008) 'Demonstrating validity in qualitative psychology', *Qualitative Psychology: A Practical Guide to Research Methods,* 2, pp. 235–251. https://doi.org/10.1080/17439760.2016.1262624

INDEX

Note: Page numbers in **bold** indicate a table on the corresponding page

For Product Safety Concerns and Information please contact our EU
representative GPSR@taylorandfrancis.com
Taylor & Francis Verlag GmbH, Kaufingerstraße 24, 80331 München, Germany

www.ingramcontent.com/pod-product-compliance
Lightning Source LLC
Chambersburg PA
CBHW050656280326
41932CB00015B/2935